tongue-lashing

Jean Kittson is a performer and a scriptwriter for stage and television. She has hosted a breakfast radio show and is a regular columnist for magazines and newspapers, now with the *Sunday Telegraph*. She is the mother of Victoria and Charlotte.

JEAN KITTSON

tongue-lashing

CARTOONS BY KERRY MILLARD

PENGUIN BOOKS

Penguin Books Australia Ltd
487 Maroondah Highway, PO Box 257
Ringwood, Victoria 3134, Australia
Penguin Books Ltd
Harmondsworth, Middlesex, England
Penguin Putnam Inc.
375 Hudson Street, New York, New York 10014, USA
Penguin Books Canada Limited
10 Alcorn Avenue, Toronto, Ontario, Canada M4V 3B2
Penguin Books (NZ) Ltd
Cnr Rosedale and Airborne Roads, Albany, Auckland, New Zealand
Penguin Books (South Africa) (Pty) Ltd
4 Pallinghurst Road, Parktown 2193, South Africa

First published by Penguin Books Australia 1998

1 3 5 7 9 10 8 6 4 2

Design by Nikki Townsend, Penguin Design Studio
Illustrated by Kerry Millard
Typeset in 10.75/14 pt Berkeley Book by Post Pre-press Group, Brisbane, Queensland
Printed in Australia by Australian Print Group, Maryborough, Victoria

National Library of Australia
Cataloguing-in-Publication data:

Kittson, Jean.
Tongue-Lashing.

ISBN 0 14 027945 8.

1. Life Skills – Australia – Humor. 2. Australian wit and
humor – 20th century. I. Title.

646.700207

To Patrick

With love and gratitude

Contents

Introduction

A good tongue-lashing is always best enjoyed between two or more people. This is a book about things I like to talk about with friends. And argue about, and laugh about and gossip about and commiserate about and gang up about and walk out of the room about and roll about about. And share. And promise never, ever to tell anyone else about.

Sometimes I've had these conversations through the intimate medium of television. (It was, incidentally, thanks to TV that I discovered one way of holding up your end of a conversation with a live TV audience is to swing over their heads on Roman rings. Especially if you use extravagant hand gestures.) Sometimes I've had the use of the gentle megaphone of radio. And some of these contributions to general discussion have been offered in the newspapers.

Is wine better than sex? Can chargrilled baby octopus damage the ozone layer? Why Barbie is good for you and your children, and nutritionists aren't. Why car sex has rules, and why the size of the car really does matter. Is it wise to go to Morocco to get a lump cut out of your breast? Is it more of a gamble than most family holidays? There's even some advice, because it's always better to give than to receive. Tips on how to handle life without getting your cuffs grubby. Even some suggestions about how to arrange your family, your furniture and your life in accordance with the principles of Feng Shui.

There are things I've been cross about and things that have made me joyful and travellers' tales and some of those medical X-files and tall tales from the marital front to swap, without which no conversation is really complete. The odd recipe. And, frankly, some gossip.

These are the views from my shoes.

It's lovely to meet you.

Jean Kittson

Get a Lifestyle

Self-assembly line

If you live in a city you'll have noticed that we don't grow our own food, we don't weave our own sheets, we don't cobble our own shoes, we don't even give ourselves full body massages. So why the hell should we assemble our own furniture? If we wanted to make our own furniture we wouldn't go to a damn furniture shop in the first place. We would buy a leather apron, some sort of tooly things and take an apprenticeship. If we'd wanted to whittle our own chest of drawers we'd have started twenty years ago with the old walnut tree out the back.

Some of us buy our furniture ready made because we aren't very good with screw drivers and, by golly, the orbital sander and router is off getting a new clutch. Perhaps our DIY kit consists of a nail file, tweezers and mascara. Try slinging together a nite 'n' day with those. How dare these furniture floggers assume we're competent to run up a tallboy out of a pile of offcuts? Were they once those obsessive, finicky children who couldn't throw balls? Who spent their weekends locked in the bedroom with a tube of glue, and an Airfix kit?

Remember Airfix kits? Tiny self-assembly planes and cars and ships that came in millions of tiny pieces you had to carefully twizzle off, sort out, stick in the right place and then paint with a single-hair brush. Not that most of us ever got that far. Most of us couldn't even open the box without getting our eyelids stuck to a co-pilot or a little topmast. And now these Airfix obsessives, these misfits, have invented self-assembly furniture as a sadistic payback for not being any good at team sports. Why do we let it happen? Why don't we explete when our new table setting for ten gets loaded into the car like a home delivery of pizzas? Does a new car get delivered as a skip full of parts and a set of spanners? Does the dentist hand us a drill and a mirror? Do we ask the butcher for a couple of steaks, and get given a cleaver and gumboots and directions to the herd in the back paddock? No!

How can we cure creeping DIY? Perhaps the next time a flat box of 107 separate pieces gets dumped on the counter, pull out of your wallet a sheet of blank paper and say, 'Here's your money, all you need is a profile of Mawson and a bit of engraving. And good luck with the hologram.'

Advice from the mysterious world of Feng Shui: The art of bringing the cosmos to your assistance by rearranging the furniture.

風水 **Alan worries that his new home's negative energy is keeping visitors away.**

Alan, from your sketch I can see that the door's in the wrong place. It's in the roof, Alan. You can counter the negative Wy Mee energies by digging an enormously long curved driveway with an ornamental lake leading right up to your place. And bang a big brass gong on the hour. Since you're on the fourteenth floor this will be a challenge, but you'll get lots of visitors, mostly from the body corporate.

風水 **Norman is concerned that visitors to his house don't appreciate his lifestyle. Should he get new friends or change his curtains?**

Norman, from the home video I can see that curtains made from old pizza containers are the work of a true individual. Unfortunately they block out the Hy Jin energies, along with all natural light. Take advantage of this. Place a heavy carved stone dragon just inside the front door. Your friends will trip over it in the dark and be in so much pain from their broken toes, they won't care what the place smells like.

The builder's friend

These new television home shows have a lot to answer for. The divorce rates in Australia have increased in direct proportion to people saying, 'No need to call Pioneer, dear, I'll concrete the driveway myself. Just like Noni did.'

Home shows are incredibly popular – more popular than soaps because unlike soaps, these shows always have a happy ending. This is totally unlike building anything yourself which not only never has a happy ending, but never has an ending full stop.

Just like children seeing sex scenes on TV, it looks a lot easier than it actually is. Watching Noni and John whipping up a window seat complete with fretwork and curved corners and stripey upholstery and doodads and dingles in three minutes flat is enough to make you try it. But the real problem is that these television shows make you think that because you *can* do it you *will* do it. When we all know the truth is that we will *never* do it.

The tiling doesn't get laid, the shelves don't get put up, the floors don't get sanded, the walls don't get stuccoed or stencilled or painted with the latest French milk paint. That's why Maggie Tabberer's show was the builder's friend. She never tried to do anything herself. She just wandered around pointing at the professionals doing their job, and then went out for drinks. The Australian way.

Just renovating the kitchen

Once the DIY home builders were pioneers, driven only by economic necessity and innocence. Then came the seventies and the birth of the New Age DIY home builder, spawned not from economic necessity but by the belief in unlimited self-expression. Away with the spirit level and a knowledge of what clay does when the rain comes. The only guidelines were personality, whim, paranoia and drugs.

An old friend, Glen, bought a very old house wedged in between a factory that made gun holsters and one that tested food preservatives on animals. It was cheap. He moved into what were the stables out the back while he renovated. The plan was to put a couple more windows in the kitchen and fix up the bathroom.

Glen started by removing just the lean-to laundry at the back of the house and then removing one of the bathroom walls to extend it enough to put in a bath. He then decided while he was at it to take out another bathroom wall and completely modernise it, ie: put in running water. When he pulled out the other two walls he realised the remaining wall against the kitchen was in pretty bad nick and what he'd do was demolish the bathroom completely and as the bathroom and kitchen shared a wall while he was at it he'd redesign the kitchen.

Glen was an extremely methodical and neat worker – some would say obsessive, I did – and he regularly took all the rubbish away to the local tip in a small trailer on the back of his car. It cost him $6 a trailer load. I mention this to illustrate the point that he thought he was doing such a small job he never even bothered to hire a skip.

After he pulled out one kitchen wall he had the idea that if he pulled down the other wall he could have a glass kitchen overlooking the garden. This crushed a lot of the garden (but never mind, the plans for the new garden were fantastic). It immediately became obvious that the third wall, behind which was a small dark bedroom, would be better removed and redesigned, allowing windows onto the garden too. This meant taking out the second wall of the bedroom, which revealed that the third wall with the one tiny window was completely inadequate and better off being rebuilt.

It then became clear that the dining room behind the kitchen's wall would be better as part of a whole open plan kitchen/family room arrangement. It too would then get a view of the garden, which was rapidly becoming no more than one trampled geranium.

After carefully removing the back wall to the kitchen to open up the dining room to the view, and taking it to the tip, the roof had started to sag over the bits where the walls used to be. Removing most of the roof was not a bad idea because it would enable the house to have a new higher roof which would allow for a second-storey bedroom to be built, thus compensating for the loss of the third bedroom which would be better as part of the whole open plan kitchen/family room area. So he removed some of the roof and took it to the tip.

It now occurred to Glen that if he built *two* second-storey rooms he wouldn't need the second bedroom downstairs, which by now was a rather tired looking room with a slight lean just across the hall from where the dining room used to be – in fact just across the hall from where the hall used to be. So he pulled it down and took it to the tip.

Next he pulled down more of the roof to allow for the second upstairs bedroom and took it to the tip too. But as he was pulling down the bits of the roof he thought he wouldn't need, the building gave a lurch and the remaining inside walls collapsed. Glen took these to the tip along with the rest of the flooring that had rotted from being without a roof for so long.

The kitchen renovations had now left Glen with one front wall supported at the back by makeshift struts looking very much like a Hollywood set. Glen then reviewed his plans and concluded that since he was renovating the back he might as well renovate the front. So he pulled down the front of the house and took it to the tip. He had taken an entire house to the tip in a small trailer on the back of his Peugeot. At $6 a trailer load he reckoned it cost him about $3000.

The good news is that by demolishing his house Glen actually increased the value of his property. He sold the site for its potential and the builders moved in.

The last time I saw him I had only one technical question: 'Why?'

Too much tool for you

They say some women marry men just like their fathers. Hah. This usually means the woman has married a drunk and didn't listen to her mother's voice of experience. It certainly doesn't apply to the daughters of home handymen.

It seems a law of nature that if your father is one of those home handymen who can find an old sheet of corrugated iron up the tip and use it to build a second storey on the house, you will marry a man who is all thumbs in the DIY department. Big, flat, black thumbs, if he's gone anywhere near a hammer. A man who will offer to glue a knob onto a toy and end up with both hands and a knob Superglued to his forehead.

Houses and toys and cars all need fixing sometime, and the other law of nature, which prevents your husband ever acquiring tiling, rewiring and knob placement skills, is the certainty that when he eventually gets round to fixing something his father-in-law will wander in and offer helpful advice. This will include the information that your husband a) has the wrong implement; b) should have done something vital first – usually involving RSJs or turning off the water at the mains or not falling off the ladder; and c) should know that the father-in-law can do that in his sleep. Or he might just stand silently watching, which is your husband's cue to drill through a pipe or step into the paint tray.

Freud should have watched husbands redecorating. Fathers-in-law always begin with contempt for the husband's tools. Who can forget the look on Paul Reiser's face in *Mad About You* when his father-in-law scorns his possession of a plumber's wrench with the words, 'That's too much tool for you?'

My husband's father-in-law recently achieved the tri-fecta. My husband was trying to squirt rubber sealant behind some wall-mounted, spring-loaded taps – a job which usually requires five hands on a good day. His father-in-law wandered in and said, 'I wouldn't use the stuff. I wouldn't put it there. And, gee, I wouldn't pay that price for it. You oughta get two for five dollars.'

If my husband hadn't had both hands wedged behind a tap and a tube of rubber sealant between his teeth, I think Dad would have been walking around making little rubber squeaking noises for quite some time.

I came, I saw, I charged

The washing machine breaks down again and you call the washing machine fixers and the bloke comes around and he switches off the switch that is called The Switch That Switches Off the Machine When the Machine is Overloaded Switch. A switch you had no idea was there because this is an old, inherited machine. It didn't come with a manual, it just came with a husband.

The bloke switches off this switch and charges you a sixty-five dollars service call fee. It is sixty-five dollars no matter what the problem. Spend three hundred dollars on a complete overhaul or switch a switch it's still sixty-five dollars to get out of the van.

Service call charges are beginning to give me a terrible case of the irrits. If you choose a career fixing washing machines, you know you will have to go to people's homes to fix them. Because most washing machines go into a house and stay there. When they break down people can't put them in the back of their car and take them to you. That is why you have a van and not a surgery. Doctors charge house calls because they do have to run a surgery and subscribe to all those two-year-old magazines and if you can't stagger there they have to leave other patients and come to you and they have to cover these costs.

It's a sting. Imagine how far you'd get if you charged your boss a fee just for coming to the office. Plumbers and electricians charge to come to your house as if you have a choice: 'Sure, I'll just dig up all the pipes and bring them around.'

Pretty soon painters will charge service calls. 'We have to come to your house to paint it. It's bloody hard work driving there, you know. That'll be seventy-five dollars before we start.' Next time anyone says there's a service call fee I'm going to say: 'Oh, don't put yourself out, I tell you what, I'll bring my blocked toilet to you.'

Dear Doctor Jean,

What can I do about tradesmen who won't tell me when they're coming and expect me to hang around the house all day?

Ida, Bowral, NSW

Ida, desperate women take desperate measures. Wait until he comes and does whatever he does. Then tell him you can only pay him one day next week, and only if you can hand deliver it. You're not sure which day, maybe Thursday, maybe the Monday after and you're not sure if you'll be there a.m. or p.m. but you're certain he won't mind hanging around his office or depot or whatever for maybe seventy-two hours, so perhaps he'd like to lay in some provisions now.

Perfect match

Why is it people will happily recommend brain surgeons, blind dates and gynaecologists but will never recommend someone to paint your house? People constantly recommend hairdressers even when you haven't asked them. Well they do with me: 'I've got this gorgeous man who touches up my tips. You need him. There's nothing he can't do with a pair of rubber gloves and a tube of mousse.'

'What's he like with drip sheets and a tub of No More Gaps?'

'So it's a relationship you're after?'

'No, I just want someone to paint the bloody house!'

Pain crosses their faces. Suppressed memories emerge of two painters with the six transistors who painted the kitchen Provence Chartreuse when they wanted Wild Corn – and whose handiwork fell off the walls the minute the door slammed behind them.

There are TV shows based on finding the perfect mate. Why don't they have them based on finding the perfect house painter? Probably because there is no such thing. Painters are a strange breed. For one thing, they move out all your furniture and move into your home. Sometimes for months at a time. They're like pigeons. First one comes and before you know it there are three or four of them. They cover everything with enormous splash mats, sit on them for days at a time, and still manage to leave white splats on everything. They can paint the same spot for hours without moving, just quietly cooing at each other.

Try saying something to them like, 'You sure that's Mellow Yellow? There's more blue in it than I expected.'

They mumble something about letting it dry before rushing to judgment and then vanish for three months. Just when you're sick of bluffing to your friends about the contemporary splash-mat lounge look ('It's very postmodern!') they're back. Slowly rolling the same spot.

It's not their fault, I know, it's the fumes. They corrode their brains, hit their nasal passages and turn into Librium Max. Or maybe the constant slow, repetitive motion of the roller going back and forth, back and forth puts them into a trance. Maybe that's what paints should be called: Torpor, You Are A Chicken and Bark Like A Dog. Till then, we're stuck with design statements like the distressed look. Painters like it. It often matches the householder's face when she sees the results.

The joy of secateurs

A woman's work, they say, is never done. And neither is a man's pruning. Why do men enjoy pruning so much? Men can prune for hours. Days. With a private smile, radiating bliss. Is it a natural extension of whittling? Is it a Zen thing? The sound of one hand clipping?

Pruning is too calm, too trance-like to be a power trip. Pruners don't leap into the air like Shane Warne as another privet falls. They smile secretly and press on. Is it the sense of working in harmony with nature, felling spare limbs like a hurricane, clearing undergrowth like a grass fire? Why do they all love it and why don't they know when to stop? Even in a small paved courtyard with a potted palm and a cactus a man finds things to prune. A man could find things to prune in a flat. The rubber plant, the vase of flowers in the kitchen, the Christmas tree. A man in solitary would prune the grout mould and move onto his toenails. Many retired men spend their days pottering in the garden, weeding, planting, fertilising and watering, nurturing foliage under the hawk eyes of their wives. The moment their wives pass on or take a discount bus tour around the casinos of Australia with their best friend, Dot, out come the secateurs, the shears and a hacksaw, and the man lets slip the dogs of pruning.

There are gardens where all that stands are the trunks of citrus trees and the Hills hoist, with one arm missing. 'They'll grow back better than ever,' declares the pruner, while his secret thought is, 'And then I'll strike again.' Is it a primal urge, a throwback response, a civilising impulse, to protect the family by clearing a space for the hut so that tigers can't lurk behind the hydrangeas and jump you on the way to the compost? So you don't poke your head through the front door for the morning paper only to have a python drop on you from the camelia? Man against nature. This packed dirt village, home, safe. That green stuff jungle, wild, dangerous. And so the buffalo grass is trimmed, the snake beans tamed, the dandelions dug up, the tiger lilies tied back, the agapanthus culled and relocated. Women shouldn't complain about pruners. Their intentions are good and in an odd sort of way, it tames their wild instincts as well, so you won't have to spend the afternoon wondering whether to ask them to paint the ceiling. There should be a book about it. Called *The Joy Of Secateurs*.

Dear Doctor Jean

What can I do about my neighbour who takes his dog for toilet breaks on my lawn?

Alan, West Perth, WA

Drink a dozen herbal teas, Alan, good whiffy ones. You'll soon be busting. Then visit your neighbour, head for the lounge room and find an open space. Adjust your clothes before leaving. Alternatively, try very small, Goodo-sensitive landmines.

Feng Shui: creating harmony with the universe by fluffing the cushions.

風水 Danielle worries about the negative energies of her hedge. It attracts the woman next door who is forever peering over it and giving advice on everything from lawn maintenance to lingerie. How can she block these yabbering energies?

Danielle, I can sense your hedge attracts the dreaded Yoo Hoo energy. There is only one way to stop Yoo Hoo from driving you Ga Ga. You must carefully place water to create abundance. That's right, install a sprinkler system along your fence. When you feel Yoo Hoo energies rearing their permed head, let it rip.

風水 Carmen wonders why her relationship depresses her now that her boyfriend has moved into the house.

Well, Carmen, from the Polaroids of your place I can see that the harmonious energy flow in your living room has been disrupted because your boyfriend built a pyramid of beer cans in it. Right next to the old Valiant engine he's taken apart on the rug. This has led to a buildup of Wan Ka energies. Just place a small bronze tortoise next to the front door to hold it open and throw the boyfriend out. You won't be happy until the Wan Ka's gone.

House-hunting season

Everyone will at some time in their lives have to search for a house. And if you are the typical house hunter you will have to undertake this search with a husband or wife. I have been looking for a house for nearly two years now. I'm an old hand. Not by choice I might add. By sheer lack of consensus. If you're having trouble agreeing on a house, remember, no matter how frustrating it is you are not alone. No matter how much you may wish you were. If you're starting out house hunting, here's a couple of things to prepare yourself for.

Rule one: If you have finally dragged your husband to a house you really like, the first thing he will do is march straight through the front door and straight out the back door, without pausing. This is normal. He will then spend five to ten minutes looking through the fence at the house next door. 'I like the house next door,' he will say. It doesn't matter whether the house next door is a mansion or an electricity sub-station, he will always say it. It will not be for sale.

Rule two: This concerns the features of the house. You will be seeing in your mind where your furniture will go. Which rooms will be perfect for children to sleep and play in. Where your husband can prove his manhood, by paying bills. Where to entertain, to work. Is the ceiling falling in? Why did the previous owners start to do something with the fireplace and then stop? Your husband, however, will be gloomily looking at the other house-hunters' cars. If there is a high proportion of BMWs or Mercedes or four-wheel drives, if he can spot several new cars or cars with dark windows or even very clean cars, he will say, 'We can't afford this house.'

My husband has a theory that if you are looking for a house on the weekend with a lot of wives who have their cardigans and jumpers draped around their shoulders instead of wearing them, the area is too pricey. He saw some women with cardigans around their shoulders and started to take off his underpants to tie them around his head, but I hurried him away.

I wonder whether husbands are like cats and dogs. Will they keep on going back to the old house until they work out where the fridge has gone?

Rule three: Then you finally go to a house auction, on site. The place is packed, although there are only about six people bidding. And the price begins to rise and rise, way past your bid and out into the stratosphere, yet nobody seems to be downcast or discouraged. Eventually it becomes a two bidder duel and one of them finally wins and the lucky couple embrace and the whole room applauds. It seems so civilised. No jealousy and no disappointment, and then you find out why. Three-quarters of the room are neighbours who have dropped in to get an idea of what their houses are worth. It is a lovely evening for almost everyone.

I've been house-hunting for the past twenty-eight months. Combing the classifieds. Driving all over Sydney. Fighting with the family. Well, I finally found the perfect house, affordable, comfortable, water glimpses if an earthquake levels the houses in front. And I missed it. It was really nice and someone else got it. It's worse than losing a boyfriend to another woman. Dammit, I've lost cupboard space to another woman. I'm so depressed. I think I need therapy for the first time in my life.

Every time the agents try to tempt me with another house, the one I lost flashes in front of my eyes. Handsome, strong, double-brick. Needs work. We were made for each other. Oh I know it had its faults – dark, brooding, squat – but it just needed the right woman.

It was there for me and I couldn't commit myself. Now it's gone! And there's another woman planning my kitchen. There'll never be another 41 Wangdorkin Road. We could have been so happy. And the great thing was my husband approved. I heard him grunt.

How to speak real estate

The real challenge in finding a house is with the creative writing skills of the real estate agents. We all knew that 'renovator's delight' in the eighties meant 'build a bonfire out of the crumbling floor timbers and throw all your money on it.' Here are some current literary pearls for the hungry home hunter:

Charming: Small. Dark. Dead geranium in pot by front door. Suit crazed loner.

Courtyard: Back door blocked by a big pot with a dead geranium in it.

Cottage: Fur on walls where previous owner attempted to swing cat.

Character: Built by an agoraphobic and redecorated in the sixties in lime green and burnt orange. The ceiling's gone and, coincidentally, the old character who lived there collected cast iron foundry parts . . . in the attic.

Family home: Pre-trashed.

Any address with an 'A': As in 24A Dump St. Someone's double-dinked their property and converted the garage into two rooms with a toilet.

Executive home: Spa with DIY plumbing in master bedroom. Walls held together with CopperArt. Mortgagee auction.

Executive home and office: Spa has fax line with DIY wiring. Mobile phone tower on nature strip.

Park-like grounds: One tree, one broken swing, covered in broken bottles and dogshit. Don't wander round it at night.

Potential: A dump. But with a new bathroom you could really make it something. Like a dump with an expensive bathroom.

Huge potential: OK, two bathrooms.

All that's needed is you and your imagination: Spend ten years paying off the bathrooms while your imagination lives somewhere nice.

Affordable: Not.

風
水 **Peter wants to know if you can employ Feng Shui to boost property values.**

Of course you can, Peter. According to the ancient wisdom of Feng Shui, you should get a few friends around, lift your house onto the back of a ute and move it to Vaucluse. This will improve your house value a lot. Also get two sets of diamond wind chimes and hang one from each ear. You'll walk and sound like the Hunchback of Notre Dame and in Vaucluse, you'll look like a local.

風
水 **Georgia wonders whether salmon pink wall-paper and mustard lounge furniture can live in harmony.**

Georgia, this arrangement unleashes the Ur Ki energies that drive friends away. Just place a two-metre mauve jade elephant in the centre of the room. This may help to distract attention.

I'll take it

My folks are moving house. After years and years in the family home. It's just an excuse to have a garage sale. I love garage sales. But after helping mum and dad I may never go to another one. Yes, you may never get rid of your broken bric-a-brac again.

We spent days deciding what to put up for sale. It's amazing how much you accumulate in twenty years. We tried to be ruthless, to cull without mercy, to sell as much stuff as possible. After being ruthless we had about three things in the market. So then we decided to put everything in the garage sale that we didn't absolutely need. Which was all the stuff we'd bought at other people's garage sales over the last ten years.

Then we priced everything, which is absolutely stupid because, on the day of the sale, no-one takes any notice of the price. They ask you how much and you say $1 and they say a dollar? And so you say fifty cents? And they say how about both wooden bowls and the raffia decanter for 50 cents and you say okay. Because the big fear is that you're not only going to be left with a whole lot of stuff you can't sell but you won't cover the cost of the ad in the paper. And there's that awful feeling that the stuff you paid good money for no-one wants at all.

It's horrible being faced with things you like that no-one will even pay fifty cents for.

But it's wonderful seeing the neighbours fall with cries of delight on something you like, which you bought at their garage sale ten years ago.

Tarting Up

Faking it

To fake it or not to fake it? It's the age-old dilemma. Whether you're talking about sex or, as was recently the case in the magazines, tans. Should we lie back, think Clarins, fake it and it's all over in fifteen minutes? Or should we insist it's real? Should we spread the towel, rub on the oil and spend the next two hours being overheated with a real chance of blisters? Not to mention rolling over every ten minutes? Well, if it's the difference between a ten-minute rub followed by a golden afterglow or every lunchtime for two months with no guarantee of anything except skin damage, then the answer is obvious. Fake it!

Let's not forget that the fashionable Natural Look is that healthy, wind-dried, après-sex look that you get from those silicone lips, bottle-blonde hair, and no sex at all because facial expressions give you wrinkles. So why not a synthetic natural tan? It's odd that the 'fashion gurus', who have no qualms about most imitations, seem to be in a quandary about fake tans.

What are 'fashion gurus' anyway? People who lock themselves in walk-in wardrobes chanting 'In, Out, In, Out'? Meditating on the possibility of life beyond lurex? Searching the catwalks for the next Chanel before the Chinese fake one?

And why aren't they giving their blessings to faking tans? Is it because, unlike facelifts and stomach staples and implants, fake tans don't hurt?

In short, the fake tan only has three pitfalls:

1. Faking too much. You fake, you finish. It doesn't seem to be working, you fake some more. You overdo it. Next day, walking down the street people say to your face, 'G'day', but to your legs they say, 'Yo bro'.

2. Only half-faking it. This is the slip, slop, slap-dash approach. The viral look you get when you don't concentrate. When you fake while watching Melrose. It's called piebald. May look attractive on a horse but on a woman it's like only shaving your knees.

3. The quickie. You slip into your cozzie. You scream. You attempt to cover up with a quick fake on the way out the door. It all rubs off. On the bus seat. Do you know where the worst place for fake tan is? On someone else's white suit.

Dear Doctor Jean,

The weekend's coming and I've got pimples. What can I do?   *Karen, Homebush, NSW*

Karen, it's grand final week. Quickly support a team and paint your face in club colours where appropriate. Two coats, use a roller, men will flock. Alternatively you may want to wait and see who's won.

Or, Karen, you can go to sleep with a face mask of humous, cucumber and lavender. Then sand it off in the morning with a sheet of number six sandpaper. If nothing else, you'll have an interesting answer when your parents bang on the door and ask what you're doing in there.

Feng Shui can guarantee your house complete celestial harmony and do wonders for your hydrangeas, but what about where you really live? Yes, that's right, your face.

風
水 Gwen fears that the Feng Shui of her face is responsible for the Rin Kli forces causing laugh lines around her eyes, mouth, ears and neck.

Gwen, is your face at one with the universe? It is very important to arrange the eyes on either side of the nose and the mouth below the nose. Try to keep the ears well apart. If your face needs a spiritual counsellor, the average nip, tuck, stretch, lower, reconstruct and polish comes in at about ten grand. Otherwise, a rollneck sweater, a big hat, sunnies and staying indoors should do the trick.

風
水 Debbie wonders whether she'd get better Feng Shui in the mornings with a new mirror.

Yes, Debbie. Hang the mirror on an up/down axis, facing the wall. Consult it daily.

Guilt trip

Look at the figures. If you don't exercise, you'll just get plump and happy. Society discriminates against plump and happy people. Look at how Bugs Bunny discriminated against Elmer Fudd. Why does Elizabeth Taylor have to pretend to be drunk and miserable? Why isn't she reading the news? And so we all pretend to exercise. We let the dog sleep on our trackies and we carry them in the bottom of our briefcases for that work-out stench, when the only burn we normally feel is spitting chip fat.

Now relax, and breathe. Just thinking about not exercising is exercising.

If you worry about not exercising, your body automatically goes into a self-defence work-out. Your abdomen muscles contract. Your breathing is more rapid. Blood rushes to your face. You flush. Suddenly you need the bathroom. The effect on your body is equal to a three-kilometre jog, only it's called guilt. Guilt doesn't require any equipment or leg room, so you can work out at work.

Caution: If you groan, bite your knuckles or hit your head on your desk people will notice, unless you are getting your bikini line waxed or you work at a bank.

Another way to exercise without exercising is called Exercising by Intent to Exercise.

Here's how to do it . . . don't get up:

One: Tell yourself you need to exercise.

Two: Tell your friends you need to exercise.

Three: Look up local facilities – pools, gyms, tennis courts, white-water rapids to rent.

Four: Find out how many people use the facilities.

Five: Try to find a place used by fewer people.

Six: Try to find out why it's used by fewer people.

Seven: Find a place to buy the gear.

Eight: Try to find a cheaper place.

Nine: Try to find people to exercise with.

Ten: Try to find a time to organise to get together.

Eleven: Make a definite time to organise a time to organise to get together at lunch.

Twelve: Work out over lunch how much time you have to exercise.

Thirteen: Work out you haven't enough time to exercise. Put it off until you have more time.

Fourteen: When you have more time, use it to tell yourself you need to exercise.

Repeat process ad nauseam. Nauseam keeps you thin. It won't give you hard step-aerobic thighs, like twin teak umbrella stands. But at least you'll have a routine.

Dear Doctor Jean,

My neighbour jogs first thing in the morning and I feel guilty. What should I do?

Amanda, Newcastle, NSW

Relax. Jogging doesn't work immediately. It will take years for your neighbour to develop wrecked knees, flimsy ankles and destroyed cartilage. But when your neighbour does, you'll still be in bed with your first delicious cup of coffee and it will be worth the wait.

Dear Doctor Jean,

Is power walking healthy?

Norma, Bendigo, Vic

Norma, jogging is a health hazard because there's nothing like the stench of a whole accounts department pounding past in a park to put you off your pie. Which leads to poor nutrition among non-joggers. But if you're power walking, you look like a one woman parade desperately seeking a brass band. Or someone who is being attacked by a slow moving swarm of bees. But the entertainment value for others makes them feel much better all day. So keep it up!

Dear Doctor Jean,

Can power walking save my marriage?

Barbara, Launceston, Tas

Oh, Barbara. The trouble with power walking is that women power walking look like drag queens walking the way they think women walk. So if your husband likes you power walking, I'd check his underwear drawer for suspenders.

Mmm . . . fat

There's been a lot of fuss lately about thin young models and the sort of impossible role model they portray to our young girls. I know my five-year-old daughter, Victoria, looks in the mirror and says she's fat and I have heart failure and think if she's like this now what's she going to be like in five years time let alone as a teenager when boys come into the picture. But she doesn't get it from young models. We can't just blame the fashion industry, that's ludicrous. She gets it from hundreds of different sources. Many of them are at home. Occasionally I might knock back another pork chop on the grounds it'll make me fat and say so. I may mention in passing that my husband's trousers seem to be getting fatter.

As a trained child psychologist, I have noticed that if you stand in front of the mirror squeezing your tummy for the Michelin effect, very soon your children will be discovered squeezing their little tummies ditto.

So let's lay off thin models. Models are thin because clothes hang off them as if there was nobody in them. Stop whining. They'll make the same clothes in your size if you ask them.

My daughter, Victoria, had a little friend around yesterday after school to play. They changed their clothes fourteen times. That's the real problem with supermodels as role models. Not being thin but believing that someone's going to pick up after them.

Naomi and the sumos

One hundred years ago a person of substance was easy to define. If you were a substantial man, you were commemorated with a statue in a park, defiantly overweight in a waistcoat. If you were a woman, to go by the photographs, your substance was measured by the size of your hat. This does not happen today, except at the Oaks and the Cup.

I write principally here of women of substance because substance is far too often confused with size and because there has been a certain amount of yittering and griping about supermodels lately and whether getting a Barbie at four will make you want to spend twenty years throwing up and the next seventy years wearing pleats.

Phooee! There's nothing wrong with supermodels or Barbies. Little girls like Barbie for the same reason that flapping frock designers like Naomi and Claudia. You can get clothes on and off them real quick. I mistrust the motives of people who whine about Barbie because she's an unreal body shape. You don't hear them complain about Cabbage Patch dolls, do you?

Barbie and Naomi are clothes models, not role models. Sydney shook for a week after the sumo wrestlers came to town. They've got fat in places where you couldn't use liposuction. You'd need a pool cleaner. And I didn't notice the men of Sydney thinking, 'Cripes! I'm four hundred kilograms underweight!' And panicking and rushing out to buy lard or become truck drivers.

Because a sumo's bodily substance is his meal ticket. And so is a supermodel's. It's what they *do*. The absence of bodily substance on a model is the same as vast blubbery rolls of it on a sumo. One gets followed by dogs in search of the perfect sapling. The other looks like volcano lava with added DNA. It's just a tool of the trade.

And the other reason I don't want Cabbage Patch super-models is because I know what fuels Naomi's ambition. She's a tall woman and it's the only way she'll get an unlim-ited supply of size ten shoes. Because if you're a woman over five foot seven, your distribution of substance requires a size nine shoe and up. And they're bloody hard to find. Naomi didn't become a supermodel to make children bulimic. She did it for the Hush Puppies.

Dear Doctor Jean,
Recently I broke my diet and gobbled down a Mars Bar. Ever since then I've had hiccups. Am I being punished?
Marlene, Epping, NSW
No, Marlene. You've just swallowed your pager.

Size matters

Whoever said size isn't important was not only polite, she wasn't talking about feet. Not mine, anyway. Size $10^1/2$. Size 21 standing together, or they might as well be when I buy them shoes. In my size, Madam will be offered lace-up Honda Civics the width of Clarke's pools. Or perhaps Madam's twin pot roasts would like something matronly in beige with a nice pump heel, as modelled by Mrs Doubt-fire. When they were younger feet, scuffing off to school, they were ridiculed: 'Hey paddles! What's on the bottom of your legs, ships?' 'Are they your feet or did your legs just grow another pair of thighs?'

Even in shoe shops: 'Have you tried the kayak department?'

All through my teens my feet were crammed into shoes two sizes too small and my bra was full of Kleenex. If only it had been the other way around.

Big feet are ugly, just ask delicate, petite, vulnerable Cinderella. Bleugh! But kids today wear black Doc Marten's lunchboxes, stuffed with Kleenex. Hurray!

Now I am older, I see the advantages of my feet. I am mature enough to realise why Barbie can't stand up. For the same reason Claudia Schiffer is never seen naked and upright. During cyclones and at cocktail parties I am the last person to fall over, landing comfortably on Claudia. And forget the girl in the ad who shares her boyfriend's jeans to stash her tampons. My man and I share shoes. Watching him sprint for the bus in a pair of Walter Steiger slingbacks, from the comfort of his Reeboks, is a very private pleasure.

There's been a lot of silly stuff in the papers about why women don't buy designer outfits any more. The usual twits say it's because women want to spend money on services rather than clothes. Phooey! The one service we don't get is people designing clothes we can wear. The reason why women don't buy top designer label clothes any more is that the clothes are bloody awful. The catwalk images that the TV news runs after the weather instead of fluffy animal stories shows what happens when a bunch of arts students set out to make women look grotesque. You'd get more fashionable, comfortable, attractive outfits out of the wardrobe for the Sydney Mardi Gras. As least at the Mardi Gras the boys have to wear the frocks themselves.

And here's a few fashion tips for the guys for autumn: Socks with shoes are back, especially in the hot weather, or if you're wondering why your personal space is getting wider downwind.

Wacky shirts with big check shorts and zany pork pie hats say: I'm the life of the party, so why are all the girls leaving with someone else?

And if you think you're ready for three thousand dollars of Hugo and Armani, remember: Women notice men who spend more on their clothes than on women. And they avoid them.

Never wear anything that will panic the cat

Fashion has always been treated passionately. Gore Vidal defined fashion as 'Knowing who you are, what you want to say and not giving a damn.' Oscar Wilde said, 'In matters of great importance, style, not sincerity, is the vital thing.' So it's just as well they never turned up at the same party in the same frock.

When it comes to fashion I always take PJ O'Rourke's advice: 'Never wear anything that will panic the cat.'

In a recent London fashion show, the so-called 'Bad Boy of Fashion', Alexander McQueen, showed off his latest Givenchy creations by turning on the fire sprinklers and soaking his models as they walked down the catwalk. It was hailed as the latest sensation, but moist models are nothing new here. It must be at least thirty years ago that Australia had its first wet T-shirt night. Possible at the Tamworth Leagues Club in the late sixties.

There are differences, of course, imitations never being quite as rich as the original. For instance I doubt whether the MC of London Fashion Week yelled out, 'Flash 'em to cash 'em!' as the models squelched down the catwalk. It's also unlikely that the Givenchy models were paid with a slab of wine cooler and two tickets in the meat tray raffle.

It's amazing just how many of these groovy, new glue-sniffing exquisites have successfully met the challenge of taking the world's most beautiful women and making them look like dorks.

If you too want to take the frock world by storm, here's how to do it at home:

For the street smart look: Go to your local Vinnies. Buy any two dresses off the two dollar rack, cut them in half and staple one on top of the other. Wear this over a boot-maker's apron or a fringed bathmat.

For the steamy seductress look: Pick up an ever popular shower curtain. Decorate it with the kids' transfers and fasten it with Velcro for that I'm-ready-for-anything-and-I'm-washable look.

Fake fur says: I care. Rip the matting out of an old Cortina, chop it up for a coat with a pair of chicken shears, then stick a fox's leg bone through your nose.

Don't forget the hat! Walk into a surgical appliance store, close your eyes, pick anything up, spray it green and put it on your head. Or if a hat made out of a truss is too con-servative, shave your head, rip the stuffing out of a horsehair sofa, leave it under a ledge where pigeons meet for a week and glue it to your scalp.

Unguent junkies

Blokes beware. Cosmetic companies are after you. Michael Jordan already wants you to believe that smelling like the stage door of his locker room will enhance your basketball. This is the thin end of a flying wedge. Everyone has skin and everyone smells of something. Men have always been happy with this arrangement. Cosmetic companies want you to be anxious about it. To become unguent junkies, like women.

Make-up is a hard habit to kick. Oh, you'll start off with a little lippy and moisturiser. You can take it or leave it. But look into any woman's bathroom cabinet. It's full of the hard stuff, sold to us by Liz Hurley to make us as irresistible as she is – although not to Hugh Grant, whose leisure activities involve women who smell like Michael Jordan's stage door. See the cleansers and toners and enrichers and calming lotions and lip creams, neck creams and nose creams. You can run a car for a year on less lubrication than the average woman uses on her face.

You won't be able to get by any longer with a bathroom cupboard full of Berocca and disposable Bics, and novelty condoms fashioned like Marj Simpson's hair. You'll need room. You'll have to re-shelve your sheds.

Make-up takes over your laundry, too. After a big night with the novelty condoms, you'll wake up with pillowslips like the twin shrouds of Turin. And mutual lip massage with your women will be out of the question. No woman is going to mix her Tropical Heat with your Pink Fit. She'll end up with a Lost Cherry that clashes with her shoes. Pubs will serve you beer with a little green straw in it. At urinals there'll be no more furtive glances comparing hose fittings. You'll compare eye bags and wonder what filler he's using on his crows' feet.

Mind you, men will probably put on make-up the way they shave; under the shower without a mirror. It'll be the same make-up job as Aunt Em, the one with the cataracts. The one who applies make-up like Pro Hart doodling on a carpet.

And male make-up will cripple those wonderful first encounters. You've met her at night, in a bar, soft light, full make-up job. But what if you get lucky and she sees you in daylight, the morning after? How can a bloke feel confident? She's told you what beautiful eyes you have. Once you'd have thought, 'You should see them with your clothes off.' Now you're thinking, 'Of course they're beautiful. They took me a bloody hour and a half.'

Dear Doctor Jean,

   Is there any cure for a hairy back?

                         Brian, Gold Coast, Qld

Brian, you are living proof that not enough men know about the healing properties of wax. There is also a simple medical procedure. Plastic surgeons will take a firm grip of your forehead and, over a day or so, stretch your hairy skin up and over your scalp, for a full, lustrous head of hair. If nothing else, it will give you one or two ideas about childbirth.

Dear Doctor Jean,

   What causes dandruff?

                         Ian, Port Augusta, WA

Sadly, Ian, dandruff is caused by worrying about your hair falling out. You'll just have to buy a silly open sports car and blend in with other balding men. The slipstream will blow the dandruff away.

Dear Doctor Jean,

   This winter I have flaking skin, brittle nails and loose teeth. What's wrong?

                         Adrian, Coogee, NSW

Adrian, you've got moths.

Head job

More than a five-hour lunch with friends, I love going to the hairdressers. Same decor, less fattening. Hairdressers make you comfortable in a soft, leather chair at a shiny, clean bench of chrome and glass in front of a huge mirror. It all feels so professional and slick and capable it makes you want to give birth.

And the salon smells of coffee and chemicals and advertising like a laboratory, the Ponds Institute perhaps. You start to believe that your colour change will not be all guesswork, well, not much. These good people are just going to play with your hair for four hours! Bliss! Great apes grooming one another give up after two hours. You are given magazines, many of them later than 1992, full of men and women with sensational hair.

'I want that one,' you say, pointing to a stunning blonde. 'Except without the moustache,' you add hastily. Easy! Flip-flop, flip-flop – they unfold a raft of colour charts. Already it's as exciting as redecorating your bedroom.

'May we suggest with your natural colour and the fascinating tonal changes around the edges . . .'

'Tonal changes? You mean grey?'

'No, no, no, it's what we call mature hair, when the colour achieves character, from its love affair with the elements – earth, air, fire, water and age. Now let's start with a base colour of Wattleseed, highlights of Wheatpollen, an overtone of Honeysun, a rooting agent of Golden Shower and about four litres of organic Peroxide.' So much science at your service. You feel if they put your head in a microwave to dry, you'd come out wearing a souffle.

A young man washes your hair, his fingers rubbing, kneading, massaging, around and around, firm yet . . . mmmmmmmm, strong yet . . . mmmmmmmmm. Ohhh yes that's what I need, a really good . . . mmmmmmmmm. Harder, harder, faster, faster, down a bit, down a bit, that's it, oh yes! Warm water spurts over your head . . . *Ohhhhh*.

Where do they learn to do that and why can't you do it to yourself? For four hours you have been fussed over: flattered and wooed, primped and preened, stroked and creamed, combed and blown. They wrap a towel around your head – you feel like a cigarette and another appointment in about forty-five minutes.

Try asking a waiter to do that.

Bottle blondes have more fun

Bottle blondes are the all-time goodtime girls. If Marilyn Monroe had stayed a brunette, she would have spent her working life as Gidget's mother or Debbie Reynolds' best friend. She would never have slept with John F Kennedy. She'd have been lucky to play Twister with Richard Nixon.

If Debra Harry had had dark hair she would never have been Blondie. She would have been Blackhead, and spent her working life as a backup singer for Gary Glitter.

If Dolly Parton had been a natural redhead instead of the bottle blonde bombshell she is, she would have ended up as the second most popular barmaid in One Horse Creek, Arkansas, singing along to Tammy Wynette on the jukebox while she hosed out the rest rooms.

If Billy Idol had remained a mousehead he would have been in gaol.

Bottle blondes have more fun, more money, more people interested in their neuroses, medication or interior design sense. Just ask Marilyn or Debra or Susan Rossiter Peacock Sangster Renouf's husbands. These famous goodtime blondes all have one thing in common: they were created by hairdressers.

There is no substitute for the professional head job. It's just not the same giving yourself one, you go through so many rubber gloves and end up with so many immoveable stains, many on your hair, and sometimes all you get out of it is bright orange split ends or a sort of greenish welcome mat on your head.

You see, the professional can look at your follicles and tell you all sorts of things you never knew – how dense you are, how thick you are, how strong or how porous you are, and all this information is used to determine exactly how much of the complex, sophisticated, laboratory-tested solution is needed; in other words: how much peroxide to use.

But the great advantage wielded by hairdresser-created blondes is that they are not born real blondes. Let's have a look at those born blonde.

The typical, classical blonde is your Nordic person. Your Swede, your Scandinavian, your Fin, your Lap, your Dane. These people for all their infamy regarding small 'l' liberal lifestyle, small 'p' perfect complexions and big 'F' easy sexuality have nevertheless NOT got a reputation for fun. They are not your goodtime girls or your party blokes. They take their roles as pure blondes too seriously.

How can you have a good time with someone whose opening remarks are, 'Lucky you. I am from the master race. Let us roll in some snow and breed and get an early night.'

They are too clean and pale and full of yoghurt.

Your German is probably the classic natural blonde. Germans do not have a reputation for being fun. Their trains go into tunnels to be punctual, not to be metaphors. Likewise, when they say, 'Let me take you to the peak,' they mean Berchtesgarten, not ecstasy. They go to bed to conserve energy, they have sex to stay regular.

But the person who has chosen to be a blonde has made a definite decision specifically to have more fun. And they'll get it because they don't have a blonde personality. They take on all the implicit sexual connotations of a blonde, by choice, when it's convenient. The sex goddess charisma of a blonde, the 'come hither' bedroom boof of a blonde, the 'do with me what you want I'm just a bimbo in it for a good time' of a blonde, *but* with the personality of, for example, the redhead. Fiery, wild, free, someone who has lived with freckles all their life and had to put up with the nickname Blue! Someone who wants to escape the fresh-faced country comfort image of a redhead, someone bursting for a good time.

Or perhaps they have the personality of a brunette: sultry, warm, rich, earthy, glamorous, sophisticated. Just add to this already very interesting person the light, bright, shiny, glorious iridescence of blonde. And you have someone who can fart, chew gum and tango divinely all at the same time.

The very act of deception is titillating in itself. It's like a masquerade ball. It gives you a certain licence to be more adventurous, more bold. It's how you feel when you wear those flamboyant, open-weave hot pants that always make you feel like raging. It's a disguise, it gives you a freedom and a percentage of diminished responsibility. Anyone who has ever been to a fancy-dress ball dressed as Marilyn Monroe, Marlene Deitrich, Madonna or Dolly Parton will remember how much more fun you had – especially if you are a bloke.

As for the partners you will attract, there is still the thrill of discovery of the truth, yet to come. While real blondes are just blonde, through and through and through.

Put simply: bottle blondes have more fun than they had in their true colours, more fun than other people who haven't taken the plunge into the basin, and most importantly, more fun than real blondes.

Let's face it. Would you rather be Bronwyn Bishop or Madonna?

My least favourite TV ad is the one flogging some lard in a jar with the ominous slogan: 'For when a simple anti-wrinkle cream is not enough.'

And certainly the model in the ad has a face so smooth you could eat off it, if the plates didn't keep sliding to the floor. But I think I've spotted her beauty secret. She's got an old pantyhose over her head, tied up at the back. There's no other explanation. So when a simple anti-wrinkle cream is not enough, just slip on a pair of old tights over your head, make them nice and tight at the back for flawless skin, and you'll also have a lovely tan.

Did you read about Melanie Griffiths? And how much she spent on her body making herself beautiful for Antonio Banderas? He works with gorgeous young beauties so to keep him off these nubile nymphets Melanie has had a $65,000 makeover. It makes me feel so guilty. The only thing I do for my man is wash my hair and pluck my eyebrows. Sometimes the other way around. Bit slack but I don't think I'd ever get nips, tucks, liposuction. I mean, what do they do with your excess lard afterwards? You could end up having a romantic midnight swim right through a big slick of it.

This is the new measurement for love. In the eighties if you really loved me you'd give up smoking or fatty foods or X-rated videos. Nowadays if you really love me you'll get a nose job or silicon breasts. Or a penis enlargement.

Brains are better than beauty

Your best feature is not your sparkling eyes or flawless teeth. It's not the rolling tundras of rich matted hair that cover your manly bosom and set off the gold locket containing your own photograph. Nor is it the spangled, early morning dew on the jogger's perfect brown. It's what pulsates behind it: your brains.

You can get by without your Mum, your Clairol, your Revlon, your personal trainer and your plastic surgeon, but you can't get by without your brain.

Without our brain we would all be seriously misinformed. The brain brings order to the chaos around us. It receives the constant data to which we are all exposed and it puts it in perspective. It eliminates the unnecessary, the unthreatening, the inconsequential. It cuts through the junk mail of life and goes straight to the cheques.

Beauty, which puts its brains on hold, even when staring into the eyes of another beauty, will never see anything but its own reflection.

The brain brings rationality. It stops ordinary everyday events such as getting older and developing brittle nails from being frightening and weird. The brain tells you decay happens to everyone. It just looks worse on others. Brainless Beauty not only lives in fear but it reigns in terror. Add the attainment of beauty is often barbaric, mostly painful, usually ridiculous, obscenely expensive and always temporary.

For instance, an important symbol of beauty in China was tiny feet. While the local brains were getting on with gunpowder and paper and astronomy and wind-dried duck, the beauty industry was working on totally dependent, vulnerable, suffering women who couldn't walk.

Remember *Wild Swans*? Young girls' feet were bound with six metres of cloth, their toes were bent inward and under and a large rock was placed on the foot to crush the arch. Girls were gagged to stop them screaming and would pass out frequently from the pain. Although the sight of women hobbling on three inch feet was considered beautiful and erotic, men rarely saw the naked bound feet which were covered in hanging folds of rotting flesh.

If brains had been prized instead, how much less trouble it would have been to hobble off and get a library card.

Nor have men escaped. For blokes in Patagonia enormous plates through the bottom lip were considered beautiful. This involved an extremely uncomfortable process and made it almost impossible to pronounce your Ps, as in: 'Please stop putting plates in my lips.' Try it.

There are even places where delicate parts of the body are covered in hot wax and then ripped off in long welts. *Aaargh!* Where anorexic fifteen-year-old girls with a bit of fuzz on their top lip are dragged off to have red hot needles inserted into the root of each follicle and then, just when they wished they'd asked for a clitorectomy instead, they get two hundred volts through the upper lip. *Wahhh!* Places like here, and now, and two whole floors of David Jones.

In the name of beauty we must endure the agony of nips and tucks, our lips plumped, our breasts inflated, our waists vacuumed, our stomachs stapled, our eyes lasered, our jowls cauterised. And after all that, Beauty wears out!

Things prey on beauty all the time and not just envious friends. The sun, the wind, the sea, the wrong face creams, facial expressions! To retain beauty we must always be fighting the things in life that destroy it – namely living, eating, drinking, breathing, grinning, giving birth, breast-feeding. All the elements essential to life are a threat to beauty – especially time.

Time acts on beauty the way it acts on a bottle of Coke with the lid off. Time acts on the brain the way it acts on a bottle of fine wine.

However wayward and unreliable the little grey cells may be, they are a greater source of comfort than the little grey hairs. As time goes by, beauty agonises over crow's feet. The brain merely finds modern teenagers loud and obnoxious.

Beauty loses its hair, its eyesight, its teeth and its taut little bottom.

The brain merely loses its interest in sex.

Beauty trembles at the onset of liver spots.

The brain merely starts to think the National Party's got a lot going for it.

The brain will get you through times of no beauty better than beauty will get you through times of no brains. And that's the beauty of the brain.

So Many Positions
So Little Time

All the best men have been taken

Why do some modern, career-minded independent women still sit around with their girlfriends over a beanshoot salad and a jug of brandy alexanders, and complain that 'all the best men have been taken'? What do they mean by 'best men'? Men so good in bed they can fold a fitted sheet? Men who won't tread on small dogs without an 'excuse me'? No. They mean men who are rich and handsome and clever, and who are Olympic-standard good listeners. Preferably in thigh boots and a cape. In short, a prince.

Feminists haven't managed to shear off the gene that makes many women want to marry up. You didn't catch Princess Di or Ivana Trump knocking back the diamond knuckledusters because they were waiting for an unemployed bouncer who could hand-roll croissants. It's because these women were brought up on stories where the heroine goes limp and is rescued by a prince: *Cinderella, Snow White, Beauty and the Beast*. How many of them ended up with Grumpy, the milkman or a talking clock, the way most women do?

If only they'd concentrated on Barbie instead of the classics. Barbie may be a plastic woman but she is her own plastic woman. She wears everything from leopard-skin jumpsuits to hard hats. She can put her feet behind her ears (just to get her jeans on). She does everything those giggling girls in the tampon ads do, and more. She skis, skates, abseils, bungee-jumps and rides horses, cars, motorbikes, dolphins – and doesn't even need a period to inspire her. She can do all this as a doctor, an engineer or a *Baywatch* babe.

Ken only comes in two flavours: plain and shaving. In 1963, Ken came as a college graduate. This line has been discontinued. Who cares if Ken's got an education? He's just a warm prop. Barbie's got all the jobs a girl's imagination can provide, plus her own diamonds and a plastic Porsche. If Barbie wants a prince, her four-year-old scriptwriter says, 'Ken, you're a prince,' and the poor dumb bastard just sits there agreeing and waiting for his chemically induced beard to grow back.

Barbie is the best role model for a girl, because the girl writes the plot. Ken only comes into the picture when Barbie gets married, during a break in the narrative. Sometimes he gets married and discarded 10 times a day. And he usually gets married in a frock.

THEY'RE ALL YOURS - I HAVE TO LIVE HAPPILY EVER AFTER

There was a fine healthy country lass quoted in one of the Easter Show colour stories. She was describing the minimum requirements for an attractive bloke. She said: 'They have to have tanned skin, no zits, big shoulders, muscular arms, no Bonds T-shirts or singlets, and Cuban or high top heels. Otherwise I won't even go over and talk.'

By golly that makes those guys that *Cleo* readers like look like a pack of wusses. You know, blonde, nice buns, great sense of humour, can strip a bok choy without bruising it. Tamworth girls use men like that to wipe down their horses after a gallop.

Have you heard about Man Check, an exciting service for women which checks up on guys before women take them out? And every man who saw it said, 'Where's ours?'

Blokes want a service that will do a full profile of the prospective girlfriend's mother. Mainly to see if she's mad. Because according to blokes, girls have a fantastic ability to bung on sanity until the bloke's in really deep, and then turn out to be just like their mum. Blokes would also like in-depth interviews with previous boyfriends and husbands. And wouldn't that have left Susan Renouf with a much smaller jewellery collection?

You are what you drive

As all single women should know, cars indicate age, economic position, marital status, the way we dress, the way we behave towards others, and our command of the 'USE YOUR FRIGGING INDICATOR YOU KNOB' English language.

If people weren't what they drove we wouldn't have a four wheel drive called a Pajero which we all know is a Spanish word meaning wanker and an English word for off-road lawyer. If people weren't what they drove there wouldn't be Volvo drivers, people permanently with the lights on and no-one at the wheel.

If I described my first boyfriend as someone who liked fishing, drank Johnny Walker and beer, not always in the same glass, and wore jeans and shirts, he could be anyone. But if I said he drove a burnt orange Monaro GTS, with a lowered front end, roll bar, wind foil and fats on the back ... Get the picture? Of course you do and you'd be right to tell me I should have got out of the car and caught a taxi.

Consider this for a moment:

Your sixteen-year-old daughter wants to go parking with a young man called Zac whom she describes as, 'Really nice, quiet and a bit shy.'

You immediately think, 'Mmm, sounds perfect. Too timid to try to take advantage of our girl.' But just before you say, 'Of course,' you stop. You can't say, 'Does Zac practise safe sex or preferably no sex, dear?' so you say, 'What does Zac drive, dear?'

What you mean is, 'Does this mobile glandular unit drive something sensitive?' For sensitive read nonsexual, like a Ford Meteor or a Mitsubishi Sigma or a Honda Civic.

(Honda Civic drivers are shy and timid alright because they know everyone else on the road has bigger bumpers than they do.)

But if Zac turns up in a purple V8 Sandman panel van – *Good God, a sin bin!* – fully equipped with a mini bar and quadraphonic sound system, wall to ceiling shag pile, tinted windows and, on the side, an airbrushed copy of a Frank Frazetta painting of 'Conan The Barbarian', standing on a rock with a swarthy, semi-naked Amazon with nipples so erect you could hang your wetsuit on them, and a sticker on the back window saying, 'If it's rocking so am I,' and another on the bumper saying, 'Don't laugh your daughter's running away to Queensland with me in this', you give one of those silent screams.

You know Zac is not a reconstructed man. He just drives a reconstructed car.

Out on the singles scene, before you know each other well enough to go to counsellors together, cars are your CVs.

If he pulls up in a white Valiant with maroon nylon seat covers, he might as well have a T-shirt that reads, 'Can my six mates come too?'

The bloke driving the MGTC who wants you to drive with him through Paris with the warm wind in your hair is married with children and having a mid-life crisis.

He is also bald and you are his surrogate for the warm wind in the hair experience. His wife will have the car, along with the house and the kids before you can pack.

And men: it is well known that a woman who drives one of those greeny-browny, rusty cars that are battered, unwashed and unserviced, the ashtray overflowing, the floor knee-deep in take-away food containers and parking tickets, and the back seat littered with tissues covered with lipstick smudges is single and is using her car as a lure, trawling it along the highways like a trout fly. Men who suffer from delusions of automotive competence are seduced by cars like these. They see the mess and think, 'Quick! Into the phone box and into my overalls, this poor woman needs help. She needs me.' Ha! In six months he'll be looking at the dings in his Commodore and she'll be saying, 'What's the fuss? I thought you were insured?'

I reserve a whole section for drivers of red cars because they are a breed on their own that transcends race, income or social status.

Red car drivers are basically assholes. The red car driver is always a little bit too fast, a little bit too cute at the lights, always cheats a little bit. The red car driver always cuts you off and never indicates. The red car is the one that always roars right up your ginger and sits there. It's always the car that suddenly appears out of nowhere when you are changing lanes and always blows its quacking little horn. They're the ones who speed when you try to pass them and slow down just after they pass you. They never let you in and yet they always push in themselves.

Just as people who drive taxis are taxis drivers and people who drive trucks are truck drivers, people who drive red cars are bloody idiots. Even my daughter knows that. I say, 'Look, darling, a red car' and Victoria says, 'Bloody idiot.' I say, 'Good girl.'

Guide to car sex

This is a guide to the etiquette of car sex. Car sex is common with young people who can't take each other home. It is also unavoidable if you have a brief interlude with someone you've just met at the lights but don't know well enough to go to a hotel.

Whatever the impulse, at least once in our lives we find ourselves in the position of having sex in a car. Usually in an uncomfortable position. Car sex requires a degree of contortion that makes Demi Moore and Michael Douglas look like amateurs. But more than flexibility, compromise and indelicacy, car sex requires rules.

Rule one: Stop the car before having sex.

Rule two: Don't park on a steep hill, whatever the view.

Rule three: Lock your doors. This is not to prevent your partner getting away. It means you won't accidentally kick a door open and turn all the car lights on.

Rule four: Avoid sex in sports cars. It's almost impossible in a Triumph Spitfire, unless you remove the windscreen. (Or so I've heard.)

Rule five: If in a sports car, always use the passenger seat. You can get wedged under the steering wheel. (I've heard that, too.)

Rule six: Even in a sedan, don't slip under the dashboard. Not only can you damage delicate instruments but you can also harm the car's delicate instruments.

Rule seven: In fact, use the back seat. Up front you could waste foreplay on the four-on-the-floor. You will also avoid confusion with the fluffy dice.

Rule eight: Don't leave the bonnet up as a ruse for pulling over to a lay-by. For the first time in your life, someone will stop to help you.

Rule nine: Don't go to sleep after car sex. It may be the middle of nowhere in the middle of the night, but in the morning it's the middle of a primary school oval.

Rule ten: Wherever possible car sex should be in a stretch limo. A fridge, a phone, TV and the sound of traffic just outside your window. But then again with these surroundings you might as well be at home with your husband.

Dear Doctor Jean,

Can you trust a man with a lambswool steering cover?
Beverley, New Farm, Qld

No, Beverley. Especially if he's given it a name.

Making whoopee

A trip through the sealed sections of many magazines reveals a world making whoopee, an international grab bag of conjugation. A map of the human temperate, tropical, frigid and erogenous zones. We first got cosmopolitan when we went out to eat Greek/French/Chinese/Nepalese. Now to be real explorers we have to stay home and do it.

At school French was a kiss with tongue, take out your gum. Now you have to take out your teeth as well. A Baguette En Escargot has become a roll in a slow-moving car. Since the *Rainbow Warrior*, the French position has involved being rammed, breached and boarded by rubber fetishists and it's all over in a minute flat.

Greek sex is a classical reference. They did great stuff with architecture. In fact, Greeks were the first people to employ the back door. At least you can smoke, if you haven't got a pillow in your mouth.

Swedish is very odd. There's not much in it for the girls, but let's just say if you've spent years doing the pencil test on your bosom, they won't be wasted.

The mags don't mention English sex, possibly because of the stereotypical Englishmen. Their definition of sexual confusion is going to a public school and not seeing anything they fancy. English sex occasionally involves women, although the rumoured sexuality of English men has always been tied up with the image of inhibited, kinky politicians who fantasise about Baroness Thatcher pulling the arms off their favourite teddy bear. Mrs Doubtfire must have been heaven. A bossy crossdresser and she couldn't even cook as well.

For women, English sex is a combination of the Pythonesque sex life depicted in 'Every Sperm is Sacred' and the Harrods and Derby Day sex life of 'Every Perm is Sacred'.

Swiss sex is also missing. Is there such a thing? The Swiss idea of a dirty night out is to ash in the bottle tops. A wild night out is hiring a girl to cross against the lights with you. Swiss sex is putting down newspaper first. Swiss romance is being as one. How was it? '2 minutes 35 seconds.' 'Ja, that's the same as I have.'

Italian sex. In true Latin tradition, the man skites about it, waving your underwear over his head, giving a blow by blow description and when he's finished telling his mother he may even come home and do it.

Finnish sex . . . Oh, I didn't know we'd started.

Dear Doctor Jean,

My girlfriend found someone else's Fleur Libras in my jeans. Can I get out of it just like the ad?

Kieran, Woden, ACT

No, Kieran. Tell your girlfriend you've always wanted to be a woman. That way when you split up no-one will be hurt.

How to handle your date without getting your cuffs grubby

Good manners are the lubricant of social intercourse, especially when dating. The time when friction is least comfortable is when dealing with boyfriends. For instance, you had two dates with Mr Not Quite Right and now you've had a better offer. How do you put him off without being impolite? Whatever you do, don't plead a headache. The chances of the old date and the new date patronising the same restaurant on the same night are one hundred per cent. The only thing to do is tell your first date that you're actually a manic depressive and your therapist wants to take you out to see if you can socialise without drugs for once. Then if the new date works out, you just dump the first one.

When you do go with your new bloke to a restaurant be careful what you order. If you order the baby duckling and he looks at you with horror and orders vegetarian, remain calm, if you can. When the food arrives, hand yours back to the waiter and say, 'Here, my good man. Release this into the wild.' Well, it's worth a try.

Ultimately, the way to a man's heart is in a restaurant. If you've been going out with a bloke for years and you want him to make a commitment, take him out to dinner somewhere upmarket and pick a really loud fight. Tears, anguish, volume, the lot. And speak clearly. Every head will turn, every woman in the place will hate him. Then tell him that if he only wants you for your body, he can have it, and start to take your clothes off. You'll be planning the wedding caterers before dessert.

Of course, there's an outside chance that you'll be alone and stripped to the waist in a fancy restaurant before dessert, but never mind, you might meet a nice maitre d'.

You may be wondering, however, what the least offensive way is to conduct a loud argument with your boyfriend in a restaurant? I can only tell you that the most offensive way to argue is to hurl glasses of wine into one another's faces. It always spreads to other tables. And remember that a carelessly flung crab claw could put someone's eye out. No, if you must share your problems with others, please put in a lot of sordid details. Give full names of third parties, and any distinguishing physical characteristics. You're on a party line, make it a party. Other diners may even take sides.

Dear Doctor Jean,

If a man takes me to dinner, do I have to go to bed with him?

Kerry, Fremantle, WA

Ah, you sweet young thing. The age-old question of first love. Of course not, Kerry. You should go to bed with him first. That way you will learn all about his table manners. Where does he put his elbows? Does he regard his food as a piece of meat, or as a meal? If you spill your drink, will he cover up the wet spot? That sort of thing. Then you'll know whether he's worth getting dressed for.

Dear Doctor Jean,

As a modern woman, what should I do if a man opens a door for me or pulls my chair out at the table?

Terese, Rockhampton, Qld

Terese, a man who pulls your chair out for you at the table is a man who will pay for dinner. However, if your principles resent the suggestion that you can't do simple things for yourself, don't get all indignant. Just follow him into the Gents and unzip his trousers for him. Then stand right behind him and whistle helpfully. He'll get the hint.

Dear Doctor Jean,

I have scored with this excellent woman. I think I love her. But how can I be sure she's right?

Barry, Crescent Head, NSW

Barry, there is a simple litmus test. Leave a roll in your toilet paper dispenser with just three sheets on it. When you check it again, if she's changed it to a fresh roll, it means she cares for other people, and she's already been through your cupboards.

Dining Mr Right

The hunger for Mr Right is as imprinted in our genes as our lust for perfect coffee. Forget what he likes in music, books, films, sport or sex. There is only one thing to look for when choosing your mate: what he likes to eat. If you like the same food, you are compatible. He's gorgeous, he's perfect, he sings like Chris Isaaks, looks like Brad Pitt and reads detective stories without moving his lips. You invite him home for dinner.

The house looks terrific in the very dim candlelight. You've sprayed Obsession on everything, including the cat. You start with chilled champagne and a bowl of freshly shucked oysters, and he starts with mineral water and a lap of freshly chucked entree. How were you to know he's a teetotaller allergic to shellfish? That's okay. Mineral water won't interfere with romance and there's always the second course. Chicken Fandango. But he doesn't eat chicken because he doesn't eat anything with two legs. 'Anything?' you reflect selfishly and hope it wasn't a waste of time ironing the sheets.

You move quickly on to the main course: Burmese lobster with glass noodles and chilli jam. It cost you a fortune and four days to prepare . . . *Oh no, is lobster shellfish?* Check photograph in recipe book. Bugger it. I'll just pick out the lobster. He'll never notice. Two mouthfuls later: 'Not chilli! My system just can't handle that much yang.'

There is one last hope, the *pièce de résistance*, or *pièce de no résistance* with any luck: freshly mangled mangoes with honey yoghurt – served in your navel. Then the swelling in his groin starts, but it's the lymph glands. Also swelling are his neck, face and head. You spend the rest of the night in casualty patting his hand, feeling guilty about the lobster.

Back home, the cat's digestive system has redecorated the house with oysters and chilli. But you have so much else in common, don't you? FORGET IT! Remember, when you're married, you'll eat together at least once a day for the rest of your lives. What about dinner tonight, love? Spag bol? Nuh. Steak and veg? Nuh. Mung beans and lentils on a bed of grated carrot? Yeah, lovely. No wonder he farts. But the most important reason to marry someone who likes the same food is that vegetarians will marry each other and make two people unhappy instead of four.

Dear Doctor Jean,

Can I trust my boyfriend?

Fiona, Fitzroy Crossing, WA

Fiona, when you next share dinner, place a single chrysanthemum in a bowl of water before his plate. If he sculls it, spits out the stalk, looks you straight in the eye and says, 'Fiona, the soup was great,' stick with him.

Arranged marriages

Many old world traditions have vanished from everyday life. Having your teeth pulled out by your hairdresser, for example. ('Some off the top and two out at the back, thanks.') Another custom all but gone is the arranged marriage.

Why? Wouldn't it be fantastic. No more months, years – okay, decades – of thinking at every party that maybe the drunk bloke from marketing could be Mr Right; that every plumber you call could be Mr Not Bad; and that every chance glance at the Laundromat could be Mr I Give Up, Near Enough. Wouldn't it be great if your mum and dad did it all for you?

You wouldn't suffer through your best years. You could be letting it all hang out – instead of wearing clothes two sizes too small and holding it all in. And it would be great for mum and dad, too. They wouldn't have to suffer at your 16th birthday party, wondering which earringed yob snorting speed in the ensuite they might one day have to call 'son'. Instead, at your fourth birthday party, they'd peer at the little innocents and try to guess through the tomato sauce which one's the future stockbroker. Then they'd have his parents over for drinks and an exchange of contracts. So civilised.

And so sensible. Mum and Dad wouldn't be led astray by your chemistry. 'One minute we were talking about how we both valued independence, the next we had three kids.'

Even better, if they leave it until your teens, then it's your mum who has to go out with the girls and drink jugs of Slippery Nipples to put her in the mood. Mum has to make eye contact and yell, 'Great band!' nineteen times before asking the contender about his superannuation plans. Mum has to keep her legs waxed and her stomach flat for years, only to find the contender isn't ready to make a commitment to her daughter.

Meanwhile Dad can go crocodile spotting in Kakadu with the lunatic greenie, and get his pecs squeezed in the crowd at grand finals with the footie freak. It'll be Dad who makes the awful discovery that the theatre buff with the nice apartment is only after his daughter for her frocks and hot rollers.

And the best part about arranged marriages is that if hubby turns out to be a disaster, you just invite your parents to move in, then take the kids and move out.

Dear Doctor Jean,

My ex-boyfriend has asked me to his wedding. What should I wear?

Amy, Inglewood, SA

Black.

Dear Doctor Jean,

Leaving the church after my wedding I realised that my husband's ex-girlfriend was there all along, wearing black. What should I have done?

Kelly, Inglewood, SA

Thrown her the bouquet. Hard. Stems out. And run very fast to the car.

Staying Together
for the Children

Wedded blitz

There was a wedding on Friday night. I know I was there because I remember hopping around the house screaming, 'Has anyone seen my shoe?' – as you do – and I know I didn't get home till four in the morning – as you do – and I'm still getting wedding cake out of my ear – as you . . . well maybe not.

Otherwise I can't remember much at all which is why I know it was a ripper wedding. A good wedding starts with the church and ends with the lurch to the taxi. Same goes for the guests.

This wedding had everything. It had the kind of ceremony that makes you cry no matter what language it's in – I love that. Some people cry because they're reminded of the romantic love they felt for their spouse on their special day, and they are reminded that romantic love is soon gone, replaced by a bond that is deeper and more profound – and I'm not talking about children. (I am talking about getting the house restumped and sharing the bill for the new damp course.)

I cried because I remembered my happiness on my wedding day, as I waved the caterers away to begin their new, richer lives together, and thought, 'Thank God it's all over!'

Getting married is an organisational nightmare. Are the flowers going to arrive? Is the food going to arrive? Is the groom going to arrive? Before the food? Next minute you hear yourself saying, 'I do. Has the food arrived?' And it's all over bar the signing of the register. You could be signing blank cheques, which is just what it's felt like so far.

This was the perfect wedding. It started off sober and formal, but soon everyone was brought together, swept up in collective embarrassment by the speech from the father of the bride. Actually a bride's responses should be, 'I do, and please no more champagne for dad until after the speeches!'

Mind you this wedding was a model of decorum compared to the first wedding I ever went to. My best friend Gwen got off with the best man and they went parking in the groom's car which was a beautifully restored Holden FJ and which was loaded full of the wedding presents. They went parking down at the local boat ramp and accidentally kicked off the handbrake, and the immaculate FJ with all the wedding presents in the back seat rolled into three metres of water. Gwen and the best man had to climb out the window and presumably flee the country.

There is a moral to this tale for impending brides and grooms: don't let the best man look after your car on your wedding night without having a couple of wheel chocks in the boot.

Dear Doctor Jean,

I'm having a hens' night and I've hired a stripper, but what other party games can we play?

Michelle, Rosebud, Vic

First, Michelle, get the stripper to perform his act all over the house while giggling guests follow him around shouting, 'Pick up those socks! We haven't got servants, you know! I'm not getting those skidmarks out! Hand wash them yourself!'

Then get the stripper to slowly and sensuously disrobe in front of you. Gather up all his clothes and iron them.

Finally, get the stripper to take off everything but his socks and then make erotic suggestions to you. Even better if he looks at his watch because he's got golf in the morning.

And if the marriage is still on, at least the bride's been warned.

Dear Doctor Jean,

This morning in bed I discovered a lump. What should I do?

Ainslie, Woolwich, NSW

Ainslie, prod it. If it farts, it's a husband.

Dear Doctor Jean,

My wife thinks St Valentine's day is just a commercialised fraud. What can I give her?

George, O'Connor, ACT

George, just give her the money and catch an early night.

A snag in your pantyhose

The sensitive new age guy, the SNAG, is still with us and generally he's an improvement. Mind you, even the sensitive new age yob is a step up from the wombat that once graced the bar stool next to you with come-ons like, 'Check the tits on you!' It was only when the SNAG was roped, married, branded and brought home that the trouble started.

I don't mean the one who reverts when hooked. The one who carries you over the threshold and says, 'The place needs a bit of a clean but you can do it in the morning.'

No, I'm talking about the genuine SNAG who cleans the house, cooks, shops, minds the children and buys little cushions for your back. This is fantastic! Unless they get carried away and tidy your underwear drawer. Where are you going to hide things then?

Okay, no-one wants to keep a man from his dusting, but there are problems. Most women have been trained by their mothers how to do housework. How to separate the clothes into whites, coloureds, skidmarks for soaking and darks. When most men do the washing it just all goes in together. Your underwear. His overalls. On a hot water heavy-duty cycle. Maybe they just like to hear a bit of loose torque? Your peach-blush silk teddy comes out like Vulcan's jockstrap. If King Gee ever made teddies that is what they'd look like.

Perhaps it's a subconscious plot to get more rags for his car? Because that's where they end up. And if you gently suggest there's an alternative, you get accused of nagging. He doesn't admit, 'I've been a fool. How can you forgive me?'

He says, 'Stop nagging.'

Give a SNAG the same advice when you're courting and he'll say, 'What would I do without you?'

Women are born with the knowledge that you don't put bone china in the dishwasher, or clean silverwear with the power sander. But how can we share this information?

The best method is to teach by example. Dry his golf balls in the microwave. Go out to the car and tinker with the engine. When he screams, 'What the hell are you doing?' tell him the car was running a bit rough so you thought you'd re-tune the carbie. And when he says you don't do it with Brasso and a circular saw, tell him to get off your back and stop nagging.

Dear Doctor Jean,

I keep finding half-empty gin bottles in my wife's shoe cupboard. What should I do?

Darren, Darwin, NT

Replace them with full ones. If she doesn't notice she may need help. And maybe you should stop dressing up in women's shoes. It could be driving your wife to drink.

Feng Shui, the art of celestial peace through arranging knick-knacks, can also bring harmony into your personal life. Many men, for example, have restored passion in their relationships simply by taking a large diamond, about the size of a golf ball, and positioning it about five centimetres from their loved one's nose.

風水 Liz wants her husband to notice her when she enters a room.

Liz, doors are in a cosmic sense the entrance to rooms. Just lower the top of the door frames all over your house. Your husband will walk into them several times daily, striking his head sharply. This will encourage him to pay attention to his surroundings. Even if he doesn't, he will be fun to watch.

風水 Karen can't sleep in her new bed since the marriage. What is disrupting the Feng Shui of repose?

From the Polaroid, Karen, one problem seems to be that your husband has one leg in the air, disturbing the harmony of your breathing. Perhaps a traditional purifying crystal will help, right up his clacker. Or just open a traditional window.

Hookers

I am from Melbourne and a devotee of Australian Rules football. A Geelong supporter who spent her formative years knitting blue-and-white head bandages for my team. But then I made an inter-racial marriage, with someone from a state I shall not name north of the Murray, and discovered that I had married into a family of hookers. My husband. His brother. His father. And his father's father, although he spent two seasons as a fly half which the family doesn't talk about.

It happens in most marriages, I think, the discovery that there's something in a husband's closet. It must be the same as discovering that you've married into the Klu Klux Klan, when you notice that all the bed sheets have to be folded a certain way and have holes in them that cannot be caused by toenails. Or marrying unsuspectingly into the Mafia and noticing that a lot of cement gets delivered, but the patio never gets finished.

Oh, there were signs. When I asked him to pass me something that was on the floor he'd turn around and crouch and sort of back foot it to me. (Luckily this technique has done our daughter no real harm. She now wants to be an astronaut.)

Earlier there was the day of our wedding reception, when the hookers retired to a back room to watch a video about a Grand Slam in 1984 and I heard my husband's voice raised in song.

A song in which he claimed that if he were the marrying kind, which thank the Lord he's not, sir, the kind of man he'd like to wed would be a Rugby half-back. This was not welcome news to me. By the time he went on to claim that he'd put it in and we'd put it in and they'd all put it in together, I was down the hall like a rocket. But when I burst through the door, they rapidly switched to 'Danny Boy'.

Now I knew that nobody in Sydney or Brisbane played Australian Rules. They still don't although some Melbourne immigrants do. So, naturally, I assumed that men in Sydney and Brisbane devoted the weekend to manly pursuits like lawn care, and sewing up the sheets and concreting the patio.

But oh, no. They used to disappear for the weekend and come back for meals reeking of alcohol, swathed in colourful scarves, with a look of pleasure on their flushed faces.

'They can't all be having affairs?' I thought.

And then one afternoon all the hookers conferred and they must have decided that if I was going to stay, it was time I was told about Rugby.

So they pointed me at the television and turned it on. And there was a man in a yellow jersey – dressed apparently for football, except with sleeves – but he was running with the ball for quite a long distance and with no bounces. Well, his feet and legs were running in one direction but his body appeared to be running in another. And he carried the football nonchalantly, in one hand, like a bag snatcher making a getaway, who wants to avoid attention.

And then he started to do a sort of dance of joy with his legs straight out, and smoothing his hair with his free hand. He danced through a lot of really large men who wanted to hurt him, but he was moving like a Ferrari doing racing skids around bollards and they missed him and then he fell over with the ball held straight out and I thought, 'I hope he's all right.'

There was the roar of a crowd on the TV and when I turned around the menfolk were on their knees giving thanks to God and screaming, 'Campese. Campese.' Which I thought was a Fiat family campervan of some sort. And then the hookers explained what I had just seen, and I was hooked.

Dear Doctor Jean,

I'm worried because my husband keeps photos of his old girlfriend in his underpants drawer. I don't want to seem jealous. What can I do?

Celia, Lakemba, NSW

Celia, hire one of those snoopy photographers to take photographs of his ex-girlfriend as she is now. Then quietly replace the earlier ones. This will remind your husband of his age as well, and why he's so bloody lucky to have you.

Last tango

Do you ever throw magazines across the room from sheer envy? I do. Not because the women are glossier or bouncier than I am. Or because Brad Pitt was born twen . . . ten years too late. But because other people's marriages seem so much more action-packed than my own.

My marriage does not experience half the ups and downs your average starlet enjoys after a Golden Globe party. When my husband was sprung in a BMW it was by the BMW salesman who told him to stop bouncing on the seats and go and look at some Datsuns instead. My latest implants were gardenias. And mine's a mixed marriage too, which is especially prone to misunderstandings. My husband's from Sydney and I'm from Melbourne. We should have as many exciting difficulties as Dannii and Juliian. Instead we have one. Although if any vigilant reporters were behind a bush within two kilometres of our house they could well misinterpret what they hear.

'Jean, put down that axe!'

'I won't, it's too hard, I hate it hard and you've made it hard again! I will not eat it hard!'

CHOP! CHOP! CHOP!

This scene occurs frequently because the main cultural difference between my husband and me is that he puts the butter in the fridge and *normal Melbourne people don't*. Why do Sydney people put butter in the fridge no matter what the weather? We don't have a butter conditioner in our fridge, we don't even have a butter shampoo, so our butter is never soft or shiny or manageable. In fact our butter is as soft and glossy as a brick.

Spread it on bread? Hah! You might just as well nail it on. The bread looks pre-chewed. It looks like it's been through the Family Court. The dog would make a better sandwich. Sure, the panting reporter would hear my husband shout, 'Just work on it until it's soft and then spread 'em gently and evenly!'

But all the paparazzi would get is a blurry shot of a woman putting butter in a microwave and setting it to 'Melbourne'. If Marlon Brando had been from Sydney, *Last Tango in Paris* would have been half an hour longer while they waited for the Norco to thaw, and he'd have got the cold shoulder, to say the least.

Dear Doctor Jean,
  Why do I dribble at night?

  Michael, Maroubra, NSW

Michael, dribbling at night is nature's way of testing your marriage. If you wake up and she's still there the marriage is sound. If she's still there and retching, tell her you often dream of her cooking. This may hold her long enough for you to investigate incontinence mouthguards.

Dear Doctor Jean,
  How can I tell my husband he's putting on weight?

  June, Halls Gap, Vic

Do unto others, that's the rule of life, June, but try to do it nicely. While he sleeps, slip downstairs and find a nice sharp vegetable peeler. When he wakes up surrounded by spuds and pumpkin with an apple in his mouth, he'll take the hint.

Dear Doctor Jean,
  I'm concerned my husband feels downtrodden and abused. How can I reassure him?

  Bronwyn, Hobart, Tas

Bronwyn, why not leave little notes for him, notes that tell him how much you care and what he means to you. A good place might be in his doggie bowl. And remember, Bronwyn, as Helen Rowland once said: 'Marriage is a souvenir of love.'

Mothers' mantra

Your dinner's on the table. Did you hear what I said? Your dinner's on the table. No, not in minute. Now! It will get cold . . . Now, I said! Turn off the telly and come in here *now*. I haven't spent all this time cooking your dinner for it to be ruined. Come on, I'm not telling you again, come and get your dinner. No, you can't eat it in front of the telly. We're going to sit down and have a normal family meal together. Did you hear what I said? Now! Will you get in here now or will I come and get you? Get in here NOW. I'm not telling you again. Right: One, Two . . . Thank you!

Geez husbands can be difficult.

Heading for the rocks?

Some ungrammatical mob from the divorce industry, called Relationships Australia, has issued a stern list of warning signs that you're heading for the rocks. Actually they're all signs of a healthy, normal marriage.

Given up joint activities? This just means you want your own space.

Feel dissatisfied and unhappy? You've kept your individuality. Well done!

An affair? This is a traditional working arrangement which finishes when he goes back to his wife, and she gets the upper hand for years.

Increased fatigue? Can't meet work responsibilities? Hey! You've both got jobs and you're drinking too much together.

Do you argue over parenting? Gee. You must be parents.

This outfit also has tips to keep your marriage together which could just as easily blow your marriage apart.

Teach each other things. This is a sure way of being told to 'get off my back'.

Keep quiet when your partner makes mistakes. Oh, sure. This leads to arguments that begin: 'Why didn't you tell me I was speeding?'

Share the load, agree on who does what around the house and then do what you enjoy the most. So the garbage never goes out.

Make time for yourself. Put your feet up. And hear someone say: 'Get off your backside and put the garbage out.'

Express your feelings honestly. Hah! This person has never been married.

What we need are helpful statistics. Like how many people who snore get divorced? Are Scorpios and Capricorns statistically incompatible? What's the divorce rate after white weddings, or theme weddings where they dress up as knights and damsels or Mickey and Minnie? My money's on the theme weddings. Any two people who share those tastes will only be happy with each other.

The three ages of sexuality

Sex! Sex! Sex! Every time you open a newspaper or magazine. I've got sex coming out of my ears. I've had it up to pussy's bow with all this sex stuff. Don't get me wrong. I have needs; I enjoy reading about sex as much as the next person. I just don't believe there's as much of it in real life, especially real life with a young family. A lot of things happen when you've got kids, and a lot of sex isn't any of them.

There are three Ages of Sexuality. The first is when you're afraid of your mother walking in on you. The second is when you're afraid of the person you're supposed to be with walking in on you. The third is when you're afraid of the kids walking in on you.

When you're in the sticky grip of the third age, not even the *Kama Sutra* helps. It starts, you'll remember, with a basic list of parts. The Yoni and the Lingam or, as we say, the Honey Pot and the Throbber. Then there's a guide to types of partners: the antelope, the elephant, the hamster and so forth. They're supposed to match.

Too late after the wedding when you discover you're a waterbed married to a water buffalo.

Lastly, instead of simple instructions, such as inset Tab A into Slot B, there's about 101 positions. The Position of the Hummingbird or, my personal favourite, the Position of the Sloth. The Position of the Gerbil is fine if it's just for two, and the only consideration is your Y ligament and his ears, but much more likely for mum and dad is the position of the Lego. That's when you revive the magic with a quickie on the rug in front of the fire. She gets a corner block grinding into her elbows and he gets a roof edge embedded in his forehead.

Then there's the position of the Giant Gippsland Earthworms. That's when the kids walk in and you pretend you're being Giant Gippsland Earthworms. This is both educational and surprisingly convincing.

Dear Doctor Jean,

I've got six kids. What's a reliable contraceptive?

Kate, Burwood, Vic

Kate, six kids ought to be a reliable contraceptive. Have you thought about using condoms? At full stretch, condoms are as strong as rubber bands and farmers tie rubber bands around lambs tails and after a while they drop off. Enough said.

Dear Doctor Jean,

We're happily married and the kids have good schools and we've got interesting jobs and the dog never bites anyone and we don't live anywhere near a tollway and the trouble is, we think we're letting the media down. Please help.

Leonie, Orange, NSW

Leonie, develop an eating disorder at once. Force your husband to wear your clothes. And get the kids to kick the dog. It's the least you can do.

Carpe Per Diem

Money is time

Let's face it, these days making money is everything.

Now, at aesthetically correct dinner tables this is considered to be an obscene remark. The best things in life are free, aren't they? Consider the sun, the song of the birds, consider the wild, glorious profusion of flowers, the sheer happiness of an infant gurgling on your knee. Consider the great jackpot of the gift of life itself.

But we only think that the best things in life are free because multi-millionaire songwriters have told us so. As have those seriously rich entrepreneurs who've put it on our tea towels. They are only offering consolation to people so poor that they think themselves lucky if they have $2.95 left over for a tea towel with 'The best things in life are free' printed on it.

But, argue the spiritually correct, all the great religions and philosophies of the world preach the virtues of forsaking money. That's what the children of the comfortably well-off middle classes believe when they're stoned enough to read the tea towels of Eastern wisdom. But they are too stoned to read the business section of the newspaper where it's reported that the tigers of the East are religiously cornering the tea towel market. We don't make tea towels here in Australia any more. We import them. And I don't think the people who no longer make them are any closer to happiness.

'A short life and a happy one.' There's another quote! Written before penicillin was discovered. But even before penicillin, the rich have always been different. They have long lives and happy ones. You bet. Look at the truly great fortunes of the last hundred years. The Carnegies and the Rockefellers and the Gettys and the Ludwigs and the Harrimans. Look at Lang Hancock. Look at Colonel Sanders. They all pressed on into their eighties and nineties because their later years were so well provided for by the graft of the first half of their adult lives. Their last, golden forty or fifty years were devoted to worry-free pleasures such as the fine artworks they bought, and the grand houses they bought, and the fabulous sex they bought, and the love of their ever extending families, which they didn't have to pay for until they died, surrounded by the smiles of people who never knew whether they would recover enough to alter the will.

And the artists who created their beautiful possessions very often died young in misery and crossness and poverty. And the purveyors of the great sex they enjoyed had a limited working life, because you can't buy desirable good looks without money, while a surfeit of money means you don't have to give a damn how you look.

And the families who surrounded their beds with love and constant attention and radiant, fixed smiles were all eaten out by anxiety over how long they'd have to keep it up. And anxiety takes years off your life.

So the rich go out with a smile on their aged faces. Sometimes because they have changed the will and left a marvellous joke behind. But mostly because they have bought with the money they made the most precious perishable good of them all. Time.

'Time is money.' That's the quote for those people who haven't made their money yet. But for those who have made it, money is time. The time of their lives. Which is, after all, everything.

My daughter, Victoria, is of the age when normally you would open a bank account for her. You'd put in a few dollars a month or whatever, and teach her the value of saving. This is no longer possible. She would put in eight dollars and lose twelve in charges by the end of the month. So Victoria carries her pocket money around in a plastic bag, like some junior biddy who's just won five dollars in ten cent pieces on the pokies.

How can these thieves, the banks, get away with it? They were the casinos of the eighties, the banks, the only casinos ever to lose money, and now they're the pickpockets of the nineties.

One thing I don't understand is why the late news shows gold prices. Who are they for? If you're seriously into gold, you know what the stuff's worth on an hourly basis. And the rest of us aren't going to eye off our wedding rings and think, 'Wow! There must be fifty bucks worth in that. First thing in the morning I'll ring the mint.'

Why don't they show the prices of useful things like the price of devon sandwiches at the school canteen tomorrow? Or mince? Or Omo futures?

There was a heartwarming story about a clever young man who was sick of the thieving banks and their lousy fees so he prowled around the Internet until he found a bank that was happy to have his money to invest and which didn't charge him extra for getting their hands on it. It's the First Technology Federal Credit Union in Beaverton, Oregon. But before you leap for the keyboard, has anyone tried this alternative? Take your money out of your account at the bank, go to the next counter and rent a bank safe deposit box. Stick your money in the safety deposit box . . . only you have the key . . . and visit it for deposits and withdrawals whenever you like, without extra fees. The annual rental will be much less than transaction fees, and state and federal taxes, and fees for queuing, and fees for admiring the bank's rubber plants, and all the other pickpocketing the banks go in for. We might be onto something here.

Net heads – the rev heads of the 90s

This is a golden age for people who really know about computers. The past twenty years for computer experts has been a lot like the first twenty years for the car industry. Imagine the car industry pioneers in about 1910.

Most of the population still rode horses. Everybody had a blacksmith or a feed merchant or a saddler in the family. But then came the car and suddenly there was an elite, a mere handful of people who actually knew what was under the damn bonnet. Who knew how to get a vehicle from A to B without a feed bag at one end and a shovel at the other. Who knew how these new contraptions worked. Why they stopped unexpectedly. How to fix them.

And just like today's computer experts, these mechanically minded sharpies could get away with anything. They could tell their customers there were mice in little wheels under the bonnets. They could charge a thousand bucks for a wing nut. They were magicians. Why, just like computer gurus, they even had their own mysterious language for what was going on. Technical words like 'gears' and the racy sounding 'crankshaft' and the mysterious, exotic 'carburettor'. And as long as they threw enough of these words into a sentence, people felt they were getting their money's worth. They could even back people into corners at parties and rave about camshafts and handbrakes and alternators until their victims offered them money or sex to stop. That was their golden age.

But then people got used to cars, to owning them and poking around inside them and taking them apart. People had their own opinions about cars. They even built cars themselves.

Worst of all, many people began to understand the secret car language and to speak it, and to challenge the expert with blunt objects when he wiped his hands on his overalls and diagnosed a worn thousand-dollar wingnut.

People became so familiar with cars that they even started mating in them. This may not literally be happening yet with computers, but home-programmed, customised, virtual reality nookie is not too far away for non-experts. Possibly even with four on the floor.

So the car experts fought back and they're having a second golden age right now, and they owe it all to computers. In the sixties and seventies, everyone could fling up the bonnet of car and recognise what was under it. Whack in a bit of oil and water. Fiddle with the carbie. Not any more. Lifting a bonnet is like lifting the Terminator's jockstrap. No recognisable moving parts. Just tiny little computers with warning signs on them. The damn things even talk back to you and whatever replaced the wingnut really does cost a thousand dollars.

Information Fatigue Syndrome

Wacko! The usual experts tell us we've got Information Fatigue Syndrome. Well, of course we have. Just think of the information you have to absorb even when you open one of the women's mags. Keeping up with Dannii's latest makeover, turnover or rollover. Discovering how to get those stubborn stains out of velour using bicarb and crushed cornflakes; learning how to make a delicious cheesecake using bicarb and crushed cornflakes; knowing what your tarot, your palms, your crystal, your stars say; finding out how to get that stubborn cheesecake off your thighs using the latest fold-up bullwhacker; and so on, and so on.

But what they really mean by Information Fatigue Syndrome is bloody computers. Okay, there's probably one around the house somewhere that you sort of know how to use, and the kids have got computers that NASA hasn't even got yet, and every time you go to pay a bill or use the phone or do your banking there's another bloody computer with a new way of doing things. These days everything's got a manual you've either lost or don't understand or haven't got time to read. Not so long ago the only tricky art of human communications was knowing which side of the stamp to lick.

And the same experts who invented Information Fatigue Syndrome have come up with the frightening information that the amount of information is doubling every five minutes like cockroaches under the fridge.

Catch up, catch up, catch up! The only people who don't care have got Alzheimer's. And the truth of the matter is that the only information that's doubling is the information about bloody computers and you'll never catch up unless you can arrange to be reborn every twelve years or so and have the eager mind of a child. Stuff 'em! Unplug the bloody thing and write someone a letter.

Dear Doctor Jean,

Am I having a nervous breakdown?

Brenda, Chidlow, WA

Brenda, you'll have to apply the simple formula E equals W over B to the power of S. That's when the Energy required to go to Work is greater than the Energy required to stay in Bed and Scream quietly to yourself. The only answer is to take a piece of paper and a pen and write down all the things you have to be thankful for, and then run outside and bark at cars.

Dear Doctor Jean,

I have a seasonal problem. My other half keeps bringing home the flu from the office. What can I do?

Meredith, Merton, Tas

Stay in bed and rest, Meredith, and while you're there, ring his boss anonymously and suggest that your other half has been going through the petty cash. He'll be home to look after you in no time.

Fresh news from the Department of Useless Information. Some highly paid expert has been sent out on a blinder of a pub crawl and has come back with the news that unemployed people drink and smoke more than anyone else – except for people who have full-time employment and work long hours. So no need to sober up when you're going for that big job, and no need to worry if you lose it. Your leisure activities are safe.

The department of Useless Information is, of course, closely linked with the Department of Whining Nutritionists. What deeply troubles these folk is that people who work hard and drink and smoke a lot aren't getting any sicker than anyone else. Wait until they find out that people who work and drink and smoke a lot also eat heaps of stodge on the run. Yep, the only real health risks in the community are the teetotalling, non-smoking, diet nags in very easy jobs, like nutritionists. They're going over like ninepins.

Stress leave

Stress leave is the grownup version of faking a temperature with a mouth full of warm water and getting the day off school. It's a caring, nurturing version of the great Aussie try-on, up there with wharfies' back and backbenchers' flu. (Hic!)

The workforce includes steeplejacks, crocodile keepers, bomb disposal experts, people who milk snakes' venom, sheep crutchers and Jeff Kennett's hairdresser (unless the last two double up). So guess who suffers the most stress? Stress counsellors.

Here, no kidding, are the official symptoms of work-related stress.

1. Can't sleep (even at your desk after lunch).

2. Nightmares about work (the third bottle at lunch was a mistake).

3. Can't pay attention at work (the fourth bottle wasn't helpful either).

4. Start to make mistakes at work (like going back to the office).

5. Palpitations, increased blood pressure and hyperventilation (from going back to the office and starting an affair).

6. Feel tired and worn out. Aches due to muscle tension. (That'll teach you to do it on the photocopier).

7. Reduced immunity to colds and flu. (Air conditioning and no knickers).

8. Migraines and arthritis. (Photocopiers are not built for comfort.)

9. Feel sick in the stomach. (Someone put up the photocopies on the noticeboard.)

These symptoms aren't stress-related, they're life-related. They can be caused by simply having things to do. Things like bringing up teenagers; queuing at the supermarket; sitting in traffic; being alive.

The first time I had those symptoms, I didn't have a job – I was going for one. Perhaps that's the next step: turn up on the first day of a new job and take sick leave for the stress you suffered applying for it.

Stress leave is such a limp fall. Life is stress. Everything is under stress – what do you think gravity is?

The only substance that doesn't experience stress is gas. You want a stress-free life? Give up stress counselling and morph into a fart.

Dear Doctor Jean,

How can I get the boss to give me Monday off after the Mardi Gras without letting on that I'm gay?

Slugger, Pennant Hills, NSW

Slugger, bluff it out. Claim a football injury. Chafing around the ears comes from scrums as well, and a lot of forwards walk like that after a hard match. Or you could just ask the boss to go with you.

Feng Shui, the art of celestial peace through arranging knick-knacks works well in the office creating harmony through stationery.

風
水
Ron worries about the atmosphere of his office. It's all very solemn and gloomy. How can he stimulate the Feng Shui?

Ron, you need to introduce some harmonious Wa Ki energies. Place a large ceremonial carp in each pocket, carry a small stone dragon nonchalantly, under each arm, and wear something yellow, an imperial, powerful colour. Bananas are good. Your employees will cheer up immediately. There won't be another funeral parlour like it.

風
水
Kim wants to use Feng Shui to enhance her confidence.

Kim, just rearrange yourself away from the till in Franklin's and into a merchant bank. Then move yourself carefully from wage earning to enormous riches, legally if possible. Place one solid gold Mercedes in your driveway and drape a personal trainer across the bonnet. Look at them a lot and feel your confidence return.

Camels are not teamplayers

Teamwork is a great Australian tradition. Look at the first European pioneers. You don't clearfell a hundred million hectares and park one sheep under every remaining tree without a lot of teamwork. And who did the average Australian pioneer trust as a team player? That's right. His blue heeler.

Anyone who's tried to run a business with the phone ringing and six other clients climbing up your leg to get in your ear will identify with anyone who has ever attempted to tell sheep what to do, unaided. 'Come here, sheep!' No response. Just a steady munch. 'Come here sheep and bunch up with the other sheep and go through that gate over there and crowd into that pen and walk up that chute and the first available shearer will see you shortly!' Not a flicker. They just amble around, bumping into things like politicians on a lunch break. But with a heeler! I whistle and you round them up, explain the uses of a gate, pen them in, dance across their backs, job done. And if you're cutting down a tree, you need a dog. A dog knows who feeds him and he won't let a eucalypt drive his meal ticket into the ground like a fence post without a warning woof.

Burke and Wills were a tragic example of defective teamwork. They passed up blue heelers for camels. Burke and Wills decided to explore a way of getting from Melbourne to Darwin in a straight, inland line. To this day no-one is sure why. There are easier ways of getting a drink. Only a team could do it. But Burke and Wills set off on camels.

Camels are large, surly, uncooperative, spitting, smelly individualists. They are not team players. The only advantage of the camel is the ability to survive for weeks without water. Not much use to people riding the camels, who can't. Ask a camel how he does it and the camel will simply spit in your eye and eat your hat.

And so Burke and Wills spent month after month squabbling their way across Australia. And when they got to the Gulf of Carpentaria, what did they do? Open a pub? Corner the souvenir market? Take photographs? No. They ate the camels, and tried to walk home. A blue heeler would have tried to discourage them, if only in the interests of a future supply of Goodos.

A good team always needs someone to point out where the other team members have gone wrong. They have team members like that in nuclear missile silos: one member of the team to go mad and want to destroy the planet, and the other member of the team to reason with him and shoot him if it doesn't work.

I'm sure there are those of you reading this who have had to shoot someone just like them.

Dear Doctor Jean,
> What is megalomania?

> *John, Apollo Bay, Vic*

John, megalomania means that you think the bus arrived this morning because you were waiting for it. This is nothing. There are people who think they're running the country just because it hasn't completely stopped. Megalomania can get you into trouble in queues if there are people in front of you. However, the true megalomaniac knows they're just minding your place. And, as the Supreme Ruler Of The Globe, you can afford to forgive them.

Dear Doctor Jean,
> One of my many problems in the workplace is being very attracted to a young man in my department, but he ignores me. What can I do without harassing him?

> *Hannah, St James, WA*

Simple. No need to cheapen yourself, Hannah. Just concentrate on your work until you're the head of the department. Then sack him.

Dear Doctor Jean,
> What do you do when your wife starts sleeping with your boss?

> *Dominic, Tweed Heads, NSW*

Dominic, remember your family pride. Make sure your wife always has plenty of clean underwear.

The usual scientific survey has suggested that people who let themselves get pushed around and bullied live longer. You know, meek people. This means that if you're getting a hard time from your boss or a bureaucrat or some boof-headed pocket dictator behind a post office counter, you can console yourself with the thought that you'll outlive them.

It might also suggest that if you want to live forever, you should make a bad marriage. Even if you don't live longer, it could feel like forever.

This wisdom reminds me of the lovely thought in the Bible that the meek shall inherit the earth. And also of what someone else – Voltaire, or Seinfeld perhaps – said, which was: if the meek do inherit the earth, it'll be interesting to see how long they can keep it.

Workaholics

There are fifty per cent fewer full-time jobs than there were ten years ago. Company executives are downsizing and globalising and outsourcing with all the frenzy of people who want to be the last ones left standing. In fact the only dependable full-time jobs left are for people who downsize other people, and for neologists who come up with words like 'downsize' and 'outsource'.

But, at the same time, those Australians who still have jobs have become a nation of workaholics. That's because ambition has been replaced by fear. It's so much easier to go that extra mile when you hear the firm's downsizing expert shout: 'Release the hounds!' Thirty per cent of Aussies now work more than fifty-five hours a week and many of us work well over sixty hours while lots more of you are probably reading this and saying: Sixty hours! Luxury! You talking about Easter or something?'

But this overwork ethic has finally been recognised by the modern corporation. Yes, Ladies and Gentlemen, welcome to the fully tax-deductible glamour and the highly motivational glitz of the Over-Achievers Awards, by invitation only, no partners.

Shortest Maternity Leave Award went to Glenda Blunt who had her third child behind the water cooler while on a conference call to London, New York and Hong Kong.

Overtime Overkill Award went to Peter Johnson for his third triple bypass in three years. The last one was in the lift. But plucky PJ kept right on working. He called for his mobile phone and insisted on local anaesthetic only. Well done!

Most Significant Contribution Award went to Frank Lowe from Lowe, Lowe and Lower when he not only downsized his section by seventy per cent but also downsized his family by ninety-five per cent. Excellent work! Just you now, is it, Frank? Good to hear! We hope to be seeing a lot more of you on the weekends.

A Posthumous Award goes to George Pastini, 45, after an unsuccessful liver transplant, during the company lunchtime fun run. His last words from the pavement were, 'I wish I'd spent more time at work.'

In fact this year saw new records achieved in several categories:

Most Cigarettes during a three-minute smoko in the loading dock: Twenty-seven.

Greatest Annual Loss of Hair – Natural or Pulled Out By Hand: Won by Alan 'Cueball' Potts.

In the **Stress Triathalon – Blood Pressure, Nervous Disorder and Alcoholism** – new highs were established in all three categories. The winner has yet to be identified. After she exploded, parts of her were outsourced five blocks away.

Dear Doctor Jean,

What do you do about fellow workers who use your coffee mug and don't wash it out?

Nina, Adelaide, SA

Nina, just soak a pair of your oldest undies in the mug between cuppas. No-one will go near your mug again. Or even near you.

Anthony Powell once said: 'Growing old is like being increasingly penalised for a crime you haven't committed.' And all too often it's a corporate crime. You turn fifty and your employers start to worry that some day soon you'll walk into work with a straw hat and pruning shears and try to corner the tuna mornay market. In some workplaces, if you're fifty, the only way to get attention is to spontaneously combust. Even then the twenty-somethings at the next desk think you're just another computer game.

But youth is no substitute for experience. At fifty, you've seen it all before, especially the mistakes. If you were forty in 1983, you've already lived through twelve announcements of an economic renaissance.

And there are fewer retrospective sexual harassment problems after the annual Christmas party. People don't throw house keys into a hat for a lucky dip. They throw snaps of the grandchildren.

Pleasure Hunting

Shopping mad

It's my favourite time of year, the pre-Christmas sales. And the Christmas sales and the post-Christmas sales and the New Year Sales and the January sales and the Summer sales. A time for shopping until your purse prolapses.

Shopping is the one activity available to humanity which gives universal pleasure. It's easier than sleeping. It provokes fewer arguments than sex. It is less of a health hazard than eating.

Compared to sex and sleeping and eating, shopping gives you a better chance of getting exactly what you want, more often. And when it comes to eating and sleeping and sex and shopping, only shopping is a perfectly good substitute for the other three.

Where would we be without shopping? Sitting at home carving Christmas presents. Throwing rocks at passing wildlife for Christmas dinner. And very short of advertising brochures falling out of the *Sunday Telegraph*, I can tell you.

But women who do most of this relentless festive shopping should remember those less fortunate than themselves. Especially the men and children who get dragged along. There's nothing more pathetic than the forlorn faces of men waiting in the little chairs at David Jones, hoping for early parole. The two questions men fear are: 'Who's this Ramona who hangs up when I answer the phone?' and 'How's this look on me? Be honest?'

Men have told me that taking your husband shopping is the equivalent of taking your wife while you play golf with the blokes. And they're right. They put you off your stroke. There are some things you just can't do while someone's watching. Shopping is one. It's as big a mistake as taking children shopping. Children in shops have the attention span of budgies. To assist women and restore confidence in the retail sector at this merry time of year, shopping centres should have two things:

Free childminding centres: Nobody shops like an unleashed woman. While the shopping centre is holding the baby, mum's shopping till her cards explode. It's impossible for sales people to compete with the brutality of four-year-olds.

'What do you think?'

'Looks very nice madam, it's your colour.'

'Gee mum, that makes your bottom look enormous.'

'Righto, we're going home.'

Free male-minding centres: Somewhere nice for the blokes. A big room with old shed decor, spare car parts scattered around, a mower that needs tinkering and a TV and a bar. The only alternative is to leave the men locked in the car all day, but it's a hot summer and they do chew the upholstery.

My new year's resolution is not to burst into tears when my very first Visa card bill appears. I've never had a credit card before and it really does give you the same concept of money as a five-year-old. You know how cute they are when they skip into a Mercedes dealership and try to buy a convertible with a ten cent piece. That's what credit cards are like. Me see, me want, me buy. You don't get frightened hauling real money out of your purse. Until later. The only reason I haven't got my Christmas Visa bill yet is because they're still passing it around the office, doubled over with laughter.

Some interfering scientists, and this is true, are actually working on a drug called Fluvoxamine: a drug that will inhibit the desire to shop.

I have no idea how they've tested this drug. Perhaps they injected a whole lot of mice with it and released them and when they came back they hadn't bought any shoes. Who knows?

Okay, you tell yourselves, we're not facing a big threat here, are we? Because if the stuff works, and stops the urge to shop, nobody's going to want to go out and buy any more of it, are they? But this news coincided with another true discovery which is a pill that induces spontaneous orgasm. I imagine when they tested this on mice it had the same effect as the anti-shopping drug. After all, with this stuff, who the hell needs new shoes?

I want it and I want it now

Once upon a time the most frustrating experience of shopping was swishing into a shop and not being able to find what you want. Especially in the big ticket range. Gold lamé slingbacks. A little cocktail number. An alarming hat. A French toaster. Virgin sesame seed body oil. A Bentley.

The front window and the shelves and the store room would be packed to the ceiling with things you didn't want, and when you asked for whatever foible or pearl encrusted gewgaw had just taken your fancy, the counter jumpers just sucked their teeth and said, 'There's not much call for them.' Or, at best: 'We can try to get one in.' And that grand liberating sense of greed and recklessness that got you into the shop in the first place would evaporate like a Chanel sample on the wrist.

Well, the modern-day version of this problem involves quite basic things. A new stove. A table. A simple towel warmer. There it is, in the window. You rush inside. It's in your colour. White. The way you always dreamed a fridge should be. 'I'll have that!'

'Certainly ma'am.'

'Do you take Visa cards wildly in debt?'

'Certainly ma'am.'

'Do you deliver?'

'Yes ma'am. If I have to carry it to you on the bus myself, ma'am.'

'I'll take it.'

'You should have it in, oohhh, six weeks.'

Because the bloody thing's in a warehouse in Shepparton or Broome, isn't it? And nobody keeps anything in the shop any more, do they? And all the shops whose windows get your impulse shopping juices going are as much use as the old style Chinese restaurants with plastic food in the window.

It's not enough to respond to demand. Shops have got to anticipate it as well. Before you even know you want it. Before your keys get locked in the car and your daughter tells you she wants to marry a bass player and your husband comes out of the closet and you think, 'I can't cope. Quick. I'd better buy a set of two metre ceramic leopards and six pairs of shoes.' And before the habit of not stocking things starts to spread down the shopping chain until, when you ask for six chump chops, the butcher's computer will tell him they're on the hoof somewhere out near Yass, and they'll be with you in a fortnight.

Downward mobility

It's like being let off the leash. No, not leaving your husband. Not the children moving out of home. Not even saying, 'Bugger it, leave the grey where it is.' Or 'Forget the wax, I'm wearing hair shorts this summer.' It's even more exciting. It's handing in your mobile phone. Hanging up the Nokia and going back to fist-fighting for public phone booths.

It's as liberating as giving up the fags. Suddenly your hands are free. You can leave the house without pockets or handbags. You don't have to panic about having enough cigarettes/batteries to get you through the night.

Best of all, there are times when you can disappear off the radar screen. Untraceable for an hour or so. Run free, sniff lamp-posts, chase cars. Have coffee without the phone ringing and the bank manager asking if you meant to overdraw.

'We know where you are,' is not an empty threat with a mobile phone. They do know where you are.

And they know how to charge, too. It's always twice as much as you think. The timed calls really add up. Especially when you ring your folks interstate and forget to press 'End'. Twenty-five dollars to say I'm on my way. That's my problem, I use it too much. 'Hello darling, have we got milk? Don't worry, I'll find out. I'm just coming in the door now.' People like me shouldn't be able to purchase mobile phones without psychological tests. Like buying firearms. Are you going to use it to replace normal conversation with loved ones? Yes. Are you going to use it when driving? Of course. I can't not answer a ringing phone. I JUST CAN'T.

And I can't just turn it off. Someone might try to ring. I ring people just to see if they rang me and I didn't hear.

And it's not just the cost of calls. There's the service fee and the connection fee and the sucked-in fee. Our phone has the analog system. It should be called the losing money by the minute system. We paid top dollars for our phone and today they are giving them away. Literally.

'Phasing out,' they say. Sounds soft and flossy. As if no-one will notice. Bet they notice when I advertise it in this week's *Trading Post*. 'To sell. Phone. Cheap. (If you don't use it.) Urgent sale. Owner moving into phone booth.'

Dear Doctor Jean,

I'm sick and tired of those messages on people's answering machines which promise that they'll ring back, and they don't. What can I do?

Julie, Brisbane, Qld

Julie, answering machine rage will be the next fad if we're not all careful. If it's a friend's machine, the next time you visit you should sneakily change the message: 'I'm not home right now, and I'll forget to ring you back. Please put it in writing.' Or: 'I can't reach the phone right now. I'm having it off with my hairdresser.' Something like that.

But the best way to get your messages answered is to claim to be from the State Lottery Office, and leave your own number.

Don't you think you've had enough?

One of the hardest things to survive nowadays is the healthy living Wowser. Wowsers promise you a long and healthy life as long as you avoid unsupervised sex, food and drink. What's the point?

Try relaxing with a bottle of wine, nowadays. It's become harder. Why? Because of something written on the back label of the bottle. And it's not the list of chemicals. After all, these chemicals aren't like the industrial strength chemicals they put into cask wine. Chemicals which also prevent rust and which read Headache 200 and Nausea 320. No, the major irritant on the back label of the bottle is that sniffy, priggish little motto which reads: Enjoy Wine In Moderation.

Well get stuffed! There are health warnings on everything from cigarette packets to bicycle seats. We've got cars that nag you to fasten your seatbelt. The country's got anti-discrimination nudges telling us what to think and ninety-nine separate health bodies telling us to eat our greens and bearded loons carping in the streets about the ozone layer. The whole country's infested with wowsers the way we used to get rabbits, and the least the bastards can do is GET OUT OF MY GLASS when I'm drinking to forget them. If you're already drinking when you read it, all you want to do is pick up that bottle by its neck and break it over its own head.

I will NOT enjoy wine in moderation unless I bloody well feel like it. I will enjoy a quick glass somewhere between the breakfast dishes and lunch. I will enjoy a four bottle lunch with a best girlfriend if the mood takes me – and because I'm an adult, after four bottles between us I will give her my car keys and say, 'Here. I'll pick a nice red. You get us home.'

I will enjoy as much or as little as the occasion demands, especially if it spills over into dinner and if I get nagged by drunken remorse over a last bottle at three in the morning, I don't want to be nagged by the bottle as well.

Most of us first drink wine when a well meaning parent gives us a small glass of wine at the table, mixed with water. That's the last time we enjoy wine in moderation for fifteen years. Fifteen years that span the teens and the twenties. Years of casks in cars, or flagons in panel vans for the mature age drinkers.

Losing your innocence and your lunch on Ben Ean, not necessarily in that order. Or on Stone's Green Ginger Wine. What would be on the back label of Stone's Ginger Wine? Please hurl dim sims in dad's stationwagon in moderation? Please rip the trousers off the pub band in moderation? I don't think so.

Wine doesn't need a health warning. It shouldn't be sold on prescription. It should be sold over the counter. Hurray, it is!

Dear Doctor Jean,

I've got little veins visible on my cheeks and my friends say I drink. What can I tell them?

Tania, Prahran, Vic

Tell them the truth, Tania. Those are not burst veins on your cheeks. They're inground eyelashes. And if your friends don't believe you, kick out the legs of their bar stools.

Wine is better than sex

A conventional image of women is that men want sex more than women, which is not strictly true. It's just that women who've tried both would rather have a drink than sex.

Wine has all the pleasures of sex without the risks. If your wine is picked from the wrong side of the hill you need only a Dispirin not penicillin. Wine has as many positions as sex. The missionary position: wafers, goblets, little towel for dribbles. Back door: hot afternoon, cold glass of wine, sitting on the stoop. On top: elbows on the table, mumbled conversation, a straw. Underneath: head on pillow, barrel with the spiggot just above your mouth.

You don't have to consider the feelings of wine. You don't always have to worry whether it can breathe. You can even make it cook. Wine improves food, sex doesn't. Sex makes you mind your manners. Wine throws them to the wind. If you share three bottles over dinner as a detour on the way to making the beast with two main courses afterwards, there are few phrases more likely to derail romance than 'Sorry. I'll open a window.' And you remember *Nine And A Half Weeks*. Sex turns perfectly good food into mulch.

Sex doesn't go with cheese.

But what of hangovers? So unpleasant, you don't get hangovers with sex. Wrong! The hangover you get from wine is something you wake up with and it lasts from eight to twelve hours depending on what you drank. Sometimes twenty-four if you wake up still drunk. It can usually be cured in a number of ways: Panadol, Berocca, orange juice, veal parmigiana and hair of the dog to match the taste in your mouth. With sex you also wake up with a hangover, it's called a mistake. It can last from five minutes to five years depending on what you promised it. A hair of the dog may put off the problem for another ten to twelve minutes but it will only get you into a lot more trouble. Better to wake up forgetting what you drank, than remembering what you went to bed with.

And women also know that sex leads to children. More sex leads to more children and more children leads to less sleep. More wine leads to more sleep.

Therapists tell us that the best sex aid apart from a partner, is our imagination. Imagine sex and you're likely to call out 'Kevin' or 'Mr Ed' in the wrong bedroom. But imagine a bottle of wine. I see bronzed and muscled bodies shiny with sweat in the warm morning sun. Lean limbs bent double. Long fingers lithe and firm and sure caress dew-spangled golden orbs, swollen tightskinned, translucent ready to burst. The heavy bunches dangle between fingers and are gently plucked and laid in glistening mounds. Then hitch the skirt and hoist the culottes and dance upon their ripe firm flesh until their essence runs dribbling, body warm between the toes and out the bung, dripping drop by golden drop or blood red nectar, such a morning, such a dance, such a sensation! It ought to be bottled.

And unlike sex, you can cork it halfway through.

Life's a lottery

The urge to gamble is instinctive. As someone said of second marriages, it represents the triumph of hope over experience. Gambling might even be genetic. We've all heard that Australians will bet on two flies crawling up a wall. It's the top game in the Darwin casino. Australia's even got preferential voting at elections. Other countries vote for governments. We vote for a win and a place.

Gambling is the ultimate expression of the human spirit, the voice within that whispers, 'It could be me!' The voice that drowns out all the other voices bellowing, 'Nuh. It's gunna be him.' It's a firm, indomitable optimism that sets humanity apart from other life forms. You don't catch fish drinking six schooners and saying, 'I'm okay to drive,' and gambling that the breathalyser will agree. You don't find sheep shouldering their way into newsagents for a couple of scratchies.

But you do find people in Japan lunging at a plate of lethal pufferfish sashimi, gambling on the chance that they alone will get the safe piece.

Or people along Parramatta Road driving a five hundred dollar car out of the second-hand car yard, gambling that the diff won't impact before they get home.

Because, now and again, we know someone who wins. We've got politicians in Canberra who haven't been caught out yet. There are NSW policemen whose tax returns didn't get challenged. There are even teenagers who didn't get pregnant.

There's the Adelaide casino where you can bet up to forty or even fifty cents a hand. There's the Canberra casino, struggling a bit because it's not such a novelty to sit in comfortable seats and watch your money disappear when you can go to the public gallery and watch parliament. There's the Melbourne casino where you don't even have to go inside. You can stay in the car park and take bets on how long toddlers can stay locked in a Hyundai family wagon before they dehydrate. In Sydney, organised casinos were illegal for too many years, but finding one was as easy as finding out the time, using the same method. You just asked a policeman, and he opened the door for you. Sydney police had a Gambling Squad, and they meant it. A full table at blackjack was known as a 'cabinet meeting.'

And the people who go to these casinos, the people who most dream of getting lucky, are the ones who've just done their diffs, lost their driving licences, and watched their teenage daughters waddle off to school in a loose-fitting tunic. Which is why they need the money.

Passing through the eye of a needle

There is a popular misconception that wealth is somehow sinful, or the cause of sinful behaviour. And that the rich will have a hot time in the afterlife while the poor ponce around on clouds drinking ambrosia and sneering at them. This is a rumour put about by people who aren't rich and who are shortening their mortal lives with the poison of envy.

In fact, chances are that the rich will have a better class of heaven as well. Of course it isn't the amount of money you've made that gets you into heaven. It's how nice you were. And no-one is better fixed up to be nice than the rich. Just take a look at the user's manual, the ten commandments:

Thou shalt have no other gods and Thou shalt not take God's name in vain: Easy for the rich. The rich don't need other gods considering what a good deal this God cut for them. When they say, 'My God!', they mean only a compliment to a close, personal friend.

Thou shalt not worship graven images: The rich don't worship graven images. They own them. A Rodin here, a Michaelangelo there . . . almost lost among the Louis XIV furniture.

Keep the sabbath: Take Sunday off? The rich can take the whole week off, that's how devout they are.

Honour thy father and mother: No worries, especially if you inherit. What's the first thing a rock star does? One up the nose and one on a house for mum and dad.

Thou shalt not kill: The biggie. Why would the rich kill? They've already got whatever they want. If they've got a grudge, they just get lawyers.

Thou shalt not commit adultery: The poor commit adultery. The rich have affairs. And serial wives and husbands. Why steal milk when you can buy a dairy?

Thou shalt not steal: Why steal when your credit's good? If the rich haven't got it, they just buy it and don't settle the account.

Thou shalt not bear false witness: Why would you when you can buy lawyers and accountants to do it for you?

Thou shalt not covet thy neighbour's ass: When you're rich, it's your ass everybody wants.

Dear Doctor Jean,
How do I get Ribena and Texta out of a new silk blouse?
Rebecca, Bluff Point, WA

With servants.

Family Outing

Mum's the word

Mothers! What wonderful people they are when you grow up. They are always there to give you support and love and muffin recipes and advice on stain removal. You go to mum first when you need advice on hair style, hair colour and hair removal, and husband style, husband colour and husband removal. They're always there when you need them. 'Hi mum, how are you? Could you look after the kids? Bob and I are going out. Thanks mum, we'll be back in December.'

My mother had one minor flaw as a mum. She couldn't stand the sight of blood or vomit or baby poo. I can't remember her changing my nappy. This could be due to my extreme youth at the time. Or maybe she paid the neighbours to do it. But I can remember her reaction to childhood injuries. As kids we were never off our bikes. We lived next door to a new housing estate. No houses, just gravel-strewn roads ribboning the paddocks. The fun! The accidents! The absence of helmets! My brother got a bee in his ear while hurtling down the hill. My sister's brakes gave up. To stop she stuck her toe in the front wheel. I tried jumping the gutter at the bottom of a hill. We staggered home in a bloody queue, screaming for our dear mother, who started screaming louder than all of us.

'Oh no! You're bleeding! Don't show me! It's awful! I can't stand it!' And she ran out of the back of the house and over the paddocks.

We had to ring up dad who came home from work and fixed us up, and rounded up mum. We tried to comfort her. 'Don't worry mum, it doesn't hurt. Look, I can just push the bone back in!'

Heaven help us if we were sick and vomiting. There was no stroking of fevered brows with pale and caring hands, no waiting up all night for the doctor, no chicken broth bubbling in the kitchen for the little invalids. Mum would take one look and run out, retching. Once again, she'd have to be rescued from the paddocks by dad and the doctor by torchlight while the kids staggered feverishly around the kitchen making her soup. To this day, I don't know how she handled actual childbirth. I'm not sure she didn't pay the neighbours to do it for her.

I was reading a book to my daughter Victoria and there was a drawn picture of a young blonde Princess Di type mother and Victoria said, 'Oh that mother is *sooo* beautiful I wish she was my mother.'

I gasped. I looked at Victoria, horrified, and she quickly said, 'Oh but you're really beautiful too, mama.'

But the damage was done. 'How could you say that?' I cried. 'After all I've done for you! Pushing and straining for thirty-six hours, the pain and the blood and the sweat and the tears. The screams as you tore from my bulging body, the hours of nursing you when my breasts were swollen and burning and ready to burst like lava-filled volcanoes. The sport I had to watch hour after hour at three in the morning! How could you say that to me?'

I didn't really, but you can see why some mothers would be pushed to it, especially when their kids are teenagers and say things like: 'What have you ever done for me?'

That's when so many modern mums get out the video and make them watch.

Those damn pelvic floors

Physical fitness alarmists rival nutritionists as nags. This week they've announced that ' . . . sit-ups are of no benefit to the post-natal woman's pelvic floor.' That's after a decade of telling you to touch your toes while breastfeeding or you'll never smuggle drugs through customs again.

I've had it up to my fallopians with the bloody pelvic floor. For those of you lucky enough not to know, the pelvic floor is the part of your body that stretches most when having babies. That includes your mouth when you're screaming, 'Bring me Pethidine! NOW!'

Before birth, the pelvic floor prevents your baby from slipping straight out. (So what's the problem?) After birth, it prevents your partner from slipping straight out. It's a bane to all women – except Lisa Curry Kenny who probably has a pelvic floor like a concrete slab in a carport. Two kids, two hundred sit-ups a day and she flaunts a fabulous abdomen and a pelvic floor with the grip of lycra.

Why give birth via our pelvic floors in the first place? Our mouths would be a better route. They're the biggest orifice in the body and what could happen? We'd just end up with a smile ear to ear and have to drink out of a bucket for a week.

Prenatal classes are obsessed by pelvic floors. They demand exercises before giving birth to make your pelvic muscle nice and tight. Why? Who wants a nice tight pelvic floor before the birth? I want a pelvic floor like a revolving door.

So we all have to do little clutching exercises. My prenatal class was told to imagine a lift going up to the eighth floor and coming down again. Imagine if your lift won't go past the first floor, going back for instructions. 'What model?' '1955.' 'Manual?' 'Definitely.' 'Slow?' 'Well yes, that's why there's a little stool in the corner for the operator.'

The one exercise that could help the birthing process is bungee jumping. Preferably on the day you're due. Instead of tying the rope around your ankles, tie it to your wrists. When you think the time's come, jump. Babies are born bungee jumpers. What do you think the umbilical cord's for? And if you jump at just the right time the baby should shoot straight out, like hitting the bottom of a sauce bottle.

... AND DR. TURNER WHO WILL BE ASSISTING ME

Buffalo hunting

Some men feel excluded when their wives give birth. Or 'experience the birthing process' as they call it down at the hatcheries nowadays. (Some women tell their men that they feel excluded from the tricky 'shaving every morning' process. They're being sarcastic.) Some men also complain that prenatal classes have nothing for them. This time they're right. No bar, no TV, no mower to tinker with while the wife gets fitted for her epidural. This is probably the fault of Sheila Kitzinger who wants women to be multi-skilled and so writes books about giving birth and hating men at the same time. She regards conception as much more painful and messy than childbirth.

Prenatal classes should warn men how *they're* going to feel during pregnancy:

The first trimester: While your partner is recovering on the bathroom floor from three months of morning sickness, you will get a burst of panic about the need for a second job. (This is known as the Buffalo Syndrome because in the old days a man's job was to bring home a buffalo to feed himself and the missus. When she started retching he realised he was going to need two.)

The second trimester: When the woman has difficulties bending, walking, sitting or lying, and relies on the comfort of home, you will be seized with an urge to paint the house. This is never quite finished by the time the baby comes, because of your second job. So the baby arrives at a home full of scaffolding and the welcoming smell of turps.

The third trimester: Towards the end of this trimester, the woman discovers that Braxton Hicks isn't a funk band. 'NO, THEY'RE REAL CONTRACTIONS. QUICK, IT'S COMING! IT'S COMING! Oh no, it's all right, they're just Braxton Hicks.' Repeated false alarms lead to hair-raising practice runs to the hospital in the car. During which you will either lose your licence or burn out the clutch and when the baby is due either the car or the driver is up on blocks.

The birth: Right after your partner has been in labour for 12 hours and she's looking forward to at least 18 years of child care on this baby alone, you'll say, 'Now we can all relax.'

Men need classes to reassure them that all this is perfectly normal. It's not especially helpful, but it's just hormonal.

Dear Doctor Jean,
What is a sympathetic pregnancy?
                    Chenille, Coffs Harbour, NSW
Chenille, a sympathetic pregnancy is one where your husband believes straight away that he's the father.

Sleeping like a baby

I needn't have worried about SIDS with my daughter Victoria because she never slept. One of the reasons she never slept was the fact that I was so worried about SIDS that I was constantly waking her up to make sure she was sleeping. I didn't mean to wake her up. Unfortunately she could sense the cold mirror under her nose, the overhead light going on and off every few minutes, the creaking footsteps, the anxious whispers, the little shakes, swapping her mattress, giving her a pillow, taking her pillow away, repositioning the bolsters so she couldn't roll over or lie on her tummy or lie on her back or lie on her side or lie down too flat, or be too hot or be too cold, or sleep too deeply or sleep at all really. She was fine. She just had bags under her eyes that made her look like Jason Donovan after a night on milkshakes.

This could also explain why two of the skills she mastered when she was old enough to walk were the ability to sleep with her eyes open standing up and the ability to lock her bedroom door from the inside.

At four she grew even more cunning. She shoplifted a CD of children sleeping from the local hippy emporium and she pinched a 'Do Not Disturb' sign from a hotel. Unfortunately she can't read, and I can always tell when she wants to nap because the house is full of sounds of whales mating, and there's a sign on her door ordering me to make up her room, in Japanese.

But before Victoria was old enough to get cunning, she was just awake. And of course the other main anxiety, apart from a sleeping baby, is a not sleeping baby. Since being a mother I have never and will never take sleep for granted ever.

I ran into a friend the other day with her baby. I beamed into the pram. 'But it's sleeping!' I whispered in astonishment.

'Yes,' the mother replied, 'She already sleeps all night.'

'How nice for you,' I said. 'Is she otherwise normal?'

Well it's hard to be gracious when you've got a child who, for the first two years of her life, wouldn't sleep. *Ever.* Sleep like a baby? Who invented that ridiculous, misleading, demoralising phrase? A photographer I bet. The only time they ever sleep is when you take them to a zoo. Show them their first elephant or ask them to face the camera and they're out like a light.

And all the information you get just makes you feel worse. 'New babies sleep an average of fifteen hours a day,' I was told. Fifteen hours! BOO HOO!

Fifteen glorious hours! Just give me fifteen minutes. I could have a shower. I could get out of my dressing gown. Oh hell, live dangerously! I could have a shower *and* get out of my dressing gown. I could have a cup of tea. That's if you're still drinking tea because there is always the suspicion that the reason your baby doesn't sleep is your diet. So you cut out anything that could be a stimulant to the baby – in other words, everything that is a comfort to the mother: tea, coffee, sugar, dairy products, wheat, meat, whisky. You would cut out oxygen to the mother if you thought that would help.

You try them in the cot, in the pram, in the baby harness thingy while you wander around the block waking all the neighbourhood dogs. You buy one of those Peruvian hammocks *guaranteed* to put your baby into a deep, primitive Aztec slumber but it only stimulates a deep, primitive chunder. You try with music, without music, with lights, without lights. You try singing, storytelling, mime, even simulating the sound of waves. You try driving to Port Pirie and back. And all through this you are trying to appear relaxed. Because a stressed mother is going to have a stressed child: 'I'm fine, it's alright darling, I'm really happy. I'm really not tense. You can stay awake if you want to. You're just not tired, are you? Are you? ARE YOU?' That's when you break down, which is a really important part of the bonding process – both of you lying there, sobbing.

Finally, hallelujah! Your baby is safely asleep in the approved position. You can go to the toilet by yourself . . . except that one arm's trapped under the baby's head and the other under its bottom and you are bending over the cot at such an angle your body looks like a planet lamp. Hot spasms of pain shoot down your back but do you move? No way. You freeze. You don't care if you need major surgery and a back brace in four years' time because for the moment your baby is sleeping. Peace. You even have a little nap yourself, standing up, eyes open, dribbling.

So if anyone reading this is planning a child in the next few years I would suggest the following preparation. Spend a week at home, getting in and out of your dressing gown about three thousand times and then have a forty-eight hour shower to see you through.

May I suggest the Goodos?

I always thought that having pets would prepare you for children. I was quite aware that children could be more demanding than, say, a dog. I knew that teaching them how to sit, shake hands, roll over and beg might help them get a job, but that when it came to food, they'd need more than Goodos. Even though they may prefer Goodos. And God knows, my daughter has eaten her fair share of dog biscuits.

What I can't understand is why children would rather eat a fur ball from down the back of the couch than a plate of lovely mashed vegetables or spaghetti bolognaise or fruit yoghurt or any of the other things children are supposed to love eating. 'Come on, just a cheese stick just for mummy, *please.*'

If a child won't eat, it won't eat. You can't prop open their mouths, get out the sink plunger and force it down, like preparing a goose for *paté de foie gras*, no matter how much you'd like to. I've got to the stage with my daughter where I wouldn't mind her eating a fur ball if I thought there was any nutrition in it.

And everyone always says, 'Don't worry, they won't starve.' But you *do* worry. You worry they will get skinny, or get scurvy, or get sick. But more than anything – when they haven't had a green vegetable or a piece of fruit in two weeks – you worry that you will be in the toilets at a busy shopping centre and your daughter will grunt so loudly a small crowd gathers outside the cubicle because they think someone is giving birth.

'What do you want for dinner darling?' you ask casually,

trying not to make an issue of food, as if eating dinner is a normal, everyday event.

'Um . . . mushrooms.'

'Mushrooms? You don't like mushrooms.'

'I do, I want mushrooms.'

Okay, so you cook mushrooms à la sceptic. 'Here you are.'

'Um . . . no thanks.'

'What?'

'I've changed my mind.' (Where did she get that from?)

'But I've just cooked them for you!'

'No thanks. I don't like mushrooms.'

'You have never tried mushrooms.'

'Yes I have! I don't like them.'

'No you haven't. Try them.'

'No!'

'Yes!'

'NO!'

'YES!'

'NOOO!'

Now I've done it! I've got to back down! She'll walk all over me for the rest of her life. What the heck, I'll just tip the mushrooms on her head. Quick, try the bribe.

'If you try one you can have ice-cream later.'

'Okay.' A tiny fragment touches her lips and tumbles to the table. 'I don't like it. Can I have my ice-cream now?'

So you serve her ice-cream sprinkled with Goodos and you eat the mushrooms. And that's the real problem: as your child gets thinner and thinner you get fatter and fatter.

Mum . . .

Here is a tribute to all mothers wherever you are, whatever you're doing:

Child: Mum . . .
Mother: Yes darling.
Child: Mum . . .
Mother: Yes darling.
Child: Mum . . .
Mother: Yes darling, I'm listening.
Child: Mum . . .
Mother: What?
Child: Mum . . .
Mother: I'm listening.
Child: Um . . . Mum.
Mother: Yes darling, I'm listening what is it?
Child: Mum . . .
Mother: Yes?
Child: Um, doesn't matter . . .

Take me home and tie me up

The trouble with children in public is that their brains are like a Lotto draw. Every now and then, a random ball of information is scooped up, dropped down a chute and pops out the little hole of their mouths. It might be your lucky number, something adorable like: 'Oh Mummy, this rose smells of strawberries.' More often, it is so embarrassing that anything embarrassing you might have done in the past involving three bottles of Stone's Ginger Wine and an impromptu strip, is nothing.

I took my three-year-old to our local cafe. It's just up the road from the children's court and is always packed with social workers. I was in the middle of my coffee and my daughter said very loudly, 'Come on, Mummy, take me home and tie me up.'

The whole place froze. You could hear the froth on the cappuccinos collapse. My jaw dropped. I tried to laugh. It came out a sob. I could hear the social workers knocking at my door.

I swear I have never tied my daughter up in her entire life. Well, once or twice, but she asked for it . . . Um . . . Look, the reason is quite simple. Victoria is obsessed with Peter Pan and, in the video, Wendy and the Lost Boys get tied up by Captain Hook. Sure, it's only a five-minute sequence in a two-hour film but my daughter really likes that bit . . . er . . .

Suddenly she changed the subject. 'My daddy's got a willy,' she informed the cafe.

'Darling, why don't you call it a penis?' I said caringly and firmly and quite loudly, hoping to gain a little kudos with the social workers while making a quick getaway.

But my daughter had to convince me it wasn't a penis. It was a willy. She did this by asking the man at the next table if he had a willy.

A friendly fellow, he assured my daughter that he did. She turned to me and said, in triumph, 'See, he hasn't got a penis.'

I don't know who was more embarrassed. It wasn't her.

Dear Doctor Jean,

I'm embarrassed. My three-year-old son looks up ladies' skirts at the supermarket.

Josie, Revesby, NSW

Oh, Josie! Never mind what people think. He's your son. Play is such an important part of learning. Make a game of it. Get down there and look up ladies' skirts with him. Explain the solar system. Tell him where he came from. It'll shock him into silence, and thin out the queue, too.

Don't ask

Is my daughter growing up or is the house getting smaller? Not only are her toys increasing in size, depth, width and acreage, but our smalltalk is growing more complicated. When she was younger and she talked about anatomy or her bodily functions loudly in public it would cause in me a sensation not unlike spontaneous menopause: hot flushes, irrational mood swing, tension and a very dry mouth. I remember taking her to the doctor's one morning. She had been sick and I nursed her through the customary long, sleepless night, force-feeding her baby Panadol, mopping her brow, fanning her, covering her up, uncovering her, muttering to myself. In the morning I took her straight to the doctor's. In the surgery Victoria said, 'Mama, I'm a little bit frightened.'

'Are you darling? What are you frightened of?' I said, thinking she was referring to the cold torch in her ears and the wooden spatula down her throat.

But Victoria looked up at me and said, 'I'm a little bit frightened of you.'

I get hot flushes just thinking about it. The doctor froze. I could read her thoughts. 'Will I ring Community Services or just the police?'

When children are younger, most of what their parents mutter is incomprehensible so they just file it away in some secret place, probably the same place they file away their parents' car keys. But when they get to four-and-a-half! We were watching *The Simpsons* together. My support role is to read out what Bart is writing on the blackboard in the opening credits. Before thinking, I read: 'I must not carve Gods.'

'Carve God's what?' said Victoria.

I went silent, looking around wildly for distractions as you do in the park during the big-dogs-mating-with-small-dogs season, when you sense the approach of a cross examination by a tiny QC who doesn't know the facts of life. Then a big moth flew into the room (Hurray!) and I hoped out loud that it wouldn't fly into the wardrobe because they eat the clothes and turn into caterpillars and you need mothballs.

'I've never seen mothballs. What are they like?'

I said, 'Well they're really tiny and hairy.' No I didn't.

'Have we got caterpillar balls?' she asked.

Good question. No answer. 'Ask your father,' I said.

She trotted away and five minutes later her father entered with a puzzled brow. 'Carve God's what?' he asked.

Party animals

Spring! Time for things to flower in the mulch and for the birds and bees to drop 'em and get cracking. And it's also time to start planning this year's children's Christmas party. Because maybe a lot of planning will mean it won't be like last year's party. It's taken me this long just to talk about it.

The key elements were:

1. Organisation: One idiot.

2. Location: The party was an open-plan affair; ie, in our local park. When I arrived at the crack of 10 a.m., the site I had planned the whole shebang around was taken by six other children's parties. I had to hoist our balloons next to the swings and slides. In adult terms this is like throwing a dinner party on the floor of a bottle shop.

3. Food: Is it stupid to lay tables with huge bowls of lollies in the middle of a public playground? Would you count your pay packet out on a pavement? Had I suffered brain damage inhaling steam from the saveloys? One sweet, small child fluttered over from the swings and asked for a lolly. Hey, it was Christmas. I felt generous and sociable, slightly heady with pink preservatives. I said, 'Okay, just the one.'

Like a seagull discovering a bucket of chips, the kid screeched, 'Hey! Lollies!' and hundreds of children fell upon my Freckles like a horror scene from Alfred Hitchcock's *The Birds*. I flailed wildly with strings of Little Boy frankfurts, but the sugar worked on the children like speed. It was no contest.

4. Entertainment: No clowns for me. Not like the other people's parties' clowns and fairies, whose entertainment had all the children rapt in quiet delight. Oh no! I went right to the top. I had Father Christmas, in a public place packed with children. He had a sack with about 20 small gifts. He went down in the first rush. Twenty children (from other parties) got presents they hadn't asked Father Christmas for, and 300 children got traumatised because Santa gave them nothing. They just got beaten off by a mad woman with saveloys. The whole park was in tears, including Santa. He works as a clown, now.

5. Alcohol: There wasn't any. When the other parents arrived to collect their kids and saw the riot, they needed a drink. I had provided a few bottles, but they were too late. I'd been there for hours.

Dear Doctor Jean,

I am five and I have a problem. For my birthday I didn't get a dolly that comes with furniture. How can I get one?

Victoria, Sydney, NSW

Victoria, your father got a dolly who didn't come with furniture, too, and so he worked and worked and worked and now his dolly has lots of furniture. So run along and ask your father. Take him a flower or something. He's a pushover.

Putting the father back into Father Christmas

A sure sign that Father Christmas is greasing his runners and putting Rudolph on steroids, ready to girdle the earth with joy, is that you're in a department store taking gift placemats seriously, and you suddenly go deaf. You go deaf, just for a second, because screams of terror echo down the escalator, blowing the Gentleman's Accessories Staff Choir off the stage.

It's the familiar problem. Another child has just been dragged into the presence of that great bestower of blessings, or denier of pleasure, the department store Father Christmas. The child has reacted like Christopher Skase hauled before an Australian court. AAGHHH!!! And why not? Big black boots, big red belly; his glassy eyes staring out of a slit in a white, hairy balaclava. (Are Father Christmases getting lower foreheads?) He looks like Jabba the Hutt decorated with yoghurt mould. The little children squirm on his lap, twisting their little hands together like rubbing rosaries. 'Forgive me Father, for I have been naughty.' Just stay there for the photo. Smile! Smile!

All year, Mum teaches the child not to talk to the local eccentric. Next thing, Mum's ordered the child to sit in his lap. This problem can be overcome by putting the father back into Father Christmas. Children are like cats. They will only sit on Dad's knee when he doesn't want them to. Father Christmas should be sprawled on his throne with his boots off and a beer in his hand, like a real father who's had a hard day with the elves.

Better yet, give him a TV with the cricket on. The children will be scaling his knee like sherpas. There may be some children who are wary of trying this because of the language it provokes at home. Tempt them further. Give Father Christmas a meal on a tray. Something runny. Bolognaise is good – guaranteed to soak and stain both jolly suit and child's clothes. If Father Christmas has a telephone in one hand and a hot coffee in the other, the child will be irresistibly tempted to creep up behind him and demonstrate the use of a loud toy in an enclosed space. For still photographs, just give Father Christmas a newspaper. That's when they'll want to hug him. And if you want to go further, and video children talking to him animatedly and loudly, I suggest he comes to work with a hangover.

Some Californian gimmick shop has released a range of mutant Barbies. There's Big Dyke Barbie, Drag Queen Barbie and Trailer Trash Barbie with the fag out the side of her mouth and the baby hanging off her hip and the peroxide hair with the black roots. Who needs them? Victoria's already got Drag Queen Barbie or Ken as we know him. He spends all his time in frocks or lashed to a table leg as an S&M Barbie. I blame Peter Pan. And who needs a Grunge Barbie? Just take any Barbie through the compost on a jungle adventure. So unless Big Dyke Barbie is more than the original Barbie with a leather jacket and a pierced nipple there's not much point. Ask Ken. He's tried it. No need to give Barbies to provocative designers for weird results. Just give them to a five-year-old. Put your ear to the door. Hear Ken say, 'Help me!'

Victoria was exhausted after a hard day workshopping Barbie and her demanding friends. She said, 'Phew. I'm exhausted. I feel about thirty-one.'

Mother's little helper

Kids come up with the most amazing questions about Santa. Questions that can confuse adults and cause distress. How to find the correct answer – one that won't cause trauma and psychological damage when they're older? One that has some truth but is sensitive to their delicate sensibilities? Here is a guide to help you over these awkward moments:

Q: What if I don't like what he brings me?

A: Only a spoilt little brat would ask a question like that. Clear off.

Q: If Santa doesn't bring me everything on my list does that mean I've been too naughty?

A: Yes. Clear off.

Q: (When confronted with Father Christmas in a department store wearing an obviously false beard and not making any toys.) **Is that the real, real Father Christmas?**

A: None of your damn business.

Q: Why is Santa so fat?

A: Because he eats little children who ask too many bloody questions.

I hope this helps you out for next year.

School rules, OK?

It is a truth universally acknowledged that a mother in possession of a five-year-old must be in want of a school. An all-girls' school as it turned out and this is how we found one.

Naturally, we wanted the best all round education. At a school that transforms its students into dynamic, stable young women with a remarkable degree of respect and affection for their parents. A school which provides a detailed sex education at the appropriate time and a guide to the unsuitability of bass players as partners. A school whose HSC results smoothly ease its students into highly paid careers. And a school that always knows where the PE clothes have been mislaid. Oh, and if the children enjoy going to school for thirteen years or so, that would be quite nice, too.

But should it be a girls' school? We'd read the surveys telling us that co-ed schools disadvantage girls, and as a former drama teacher I knew this to be true. I'd been one of the disadvantages. Not only because I was trained in the progressive seventies when discipline was a ten-letter word, or eight letters if you spelt it phonetically, spelling and literacy being, like, really oppressive. But because the boys took all my attention and time. Not disciplining them, just being aware of their needs. Particularly their need to sit down and shut up! Of my teaching I can only hope that some of my students can still successfully imagine themselves to be a banana and that this has been valuable to them in their careers. I have also come to the conclusion that no child of mine should ever be taught by a teacher like me.

Of course I had wider experience of schools than as a teacher. I was also a schoolgirl. I attended co-ed schools until year ten, then my parents decided that after ten years of school I had better start getting an education, and I went to a girls' school. The surfing high school I left was rough, extremely rough. The boys couldn't spell sexual harassment but they could pass any prac exam. They'd stick their hands up our dresses or press against our breasts or just punch us in the arm. The multi-skilled ones did all three at once. This showed you that you were attractive to the boys, which made you popular with the girls. It isn't just competition with the boys that makes co-ed school difficult, it's competition among the girls for the boys that brings out the claws.

I discovered to my astonishment that my new girls' school had young women who liked to learn, not just practise preliminary mating. Not so preliminary in some cases. At my old school you were not only excused if you had your period, you could leave the room if your contractions had begun.

But I wasn't socialised for my new school. My first class was Maths, the teacher was extremely elderly, nudging forty, what a pushover! I knew how to demolish her. I had a great trick to impress the boys – I could turn my eyelids inside out. I tried it on the girls. All I got were scowls. This strangely, was a relief. I realised it was much easier on the mind just to learn. Much easier on the sensitive skin around my eyes too. I also realised my new peer group pressure was to shut up and listen or be rolled in the playground later.

So a girls' secondary school seemed the right thing to do for our darling. But a girls' primary school? Did I want our daughter to be completely sheltered from boys? To miss out on social skills such as kiss chasey? After all, I reasoned, if she observes little boys in their formative years she'll recognise them in the boardroom later, when she's grown up but they haven't. On the other hand, what if she enters the workforce without ever having seen them bully, shout and stick pencils up their nose? Perhaps she won't be at all tolerant. She might say: 'Stop being such a goose' the way the girls' school students did to me.

However, I reasoned, remember your own first day at a co-ed primary school, happy to be there, smiling at a boy from a bigger class, and he punched you in the stomach. It was such a valuable life experience. Could I deny my daughter this kind of social contact? Yes.

So I decided on a girls' school. Victoria appears to love it. Naturally she tells us nothing whatsoever. We have to pick up little signs such as the fact that she came home yesterday and she could read. The day before she couldn't.

Some days she goes to aftercare, which the school opens to the boys from a nearby primary school. As I was still concerned about her unfamiliarity with boys, I asked her how she got on with the boys in the group. And she said, 'Good. We chase them and I kiss them.'

So someone knows what she's doing.

Dear Doctor Jean,
Can adults catch headlice from each other?
Gillian, Katoomba, NSW

Yes, Gillian, they can. But only before marriage, in most women's experience.

First day at school. The tears, the trauma – *oh, they're growing up* – the hugs that can't let go. And then Victoria turned to her new teacher and said, 'Can you get mum out of here? This is embarrassing.'

Three weeks later and it's been a wonderful educational experience. Mostly for me. My Latin's coming along. I've been trying to translate Victoria's school motto on her T-shirt. I think it means, 'To Infinity And Beyond.' Or possible, 'Hand Wash Only.'

Most of all, we're all learning communication skills.

'How was school?'

'Good.'

'What did you do today?'

'Things.'

'Did you eat your lunch?'

'Don't know.'

'Where's your other gym shoe?'

'Good.'

Soon I'll be able to ask her all about computers.

Lipsticks and stones

This week's study from the Department of The Bleedin' Obvious reveals that schoolgirls are worse bullies than schoolboys. Boys use brute force, until they're beaten into submission by gender roles studies. Girls are above that. Girls have cruelty. Bully boys employ techniques like The Headlock, The Squirrel Grip, The Flying Missile, The Scuffle, The Punch In The Face and the Brawl.

The bully girls' armoury is so sophisticated their battles go undetected. Here are some of the bullying techniques your daughter may confront.

Direct assaults

The Bette Davis: this mortal wound is inflicted by a best friend, no scuffle, no cracked ribs, just the deadly hiss, 'You're not our friend any more.'

The Madonna: 'Do you smoke? No? You're a dag, rack off!'

The Naomi Campbell: We're not hanging around with anyone fat.'

The more subtle assaults

The closed ranks technique: This is valuable training for adult networking. There's a circle of girls chatting about boys, gossiping about girls, comparing hair and doing lunch. (Doing lunch in the playground means swapping your Vegemite sandwiches for someone else's devon.) One day, the circle closes. The victim circles the circle, trying to get in, like the runt of the litter trying to get a nipple. What happened? One day you're happily ganging up on some poor girl because her fringe is too short. Next minute it's you. Because your fringe is too long.

The seagull attack: Girls in playgrounds are like a flock of wheeling birds. First one's the leader then, suddenly, for no obvious reason, they turn and tear the leader's eyes out, screeching behind someone else.

The giggle exclusion zone: All the girls start giggling. You giggle too, waiting to be told the joke. No-one tells you. Then the realisation creeps up on you like a drunk in a dark lane. They're laughing about you. And you don't know why. And half the time neither do they. They're giggling from relief that it's not them.

The galloping whisper: This one's a must for all future politicians. A whisper scurries around the room like a rat. The girls stare at you as if word's out that you eat your own vomit. (More likely someone's said you like Nutella.) Untrue but deadly.

These torments can make you strong. If you survive a day of this persecution without bursting into tears you will be strong enough to do the same thing to someone else tomorrow.

God stuff

Victoria's been getting some basic religious instruction at school and I think one or two points might be made clearer for the under sixes.

For instance, she asked, the way children do: 'Is dad going to die before you do?' Which is no way to talk in front of a father with a birthday coming up.

Then she explained: 'Because today we talked about our Father who art in heaven.'

And *her* father explained that he personally was hoping for around another fifty years of earthly existence if that was okay. And he suddenly felt like getting a lot of vitamins for his birthday. He also explained to Victoria that the Father who art in heaven is more of a universal concept which applies to a deity called Harold. As in *Harold be thy name*. Which we all rather hoped Victoria would explain to the rest of the class.

There were more questions, however.

'Did God die?' she asked.

'No. God doesn't die.'

'So what's he doing in heaven?'

'He lives there.'

Then there was a bit of a pause.

'Jesus and his mother, were they the first people?'

'No, that was Adam and Eve.'

A great smile of recognition.

'Oh, yes, the Addams family.'

So if all the other kids are singing *Rock of Ages* and she's doing the Addams family theme song, that's why.

Click, click.

Victoria had a clown at her birthday party last time and some of her friends have had fairies and I won't say anything about a typical Sydney party needing both. But for her next birthday party, some months off, Victoria had an inspiration that other birthday girls are going to find hard to match. She's asking God to come. That's *the* God. The omnipotent one. Creator of all being. Weddings, parties, everything.

God is going to provide the entertainment and, with any luck, given His skills, He'll provide the catering and get the chocolate crackles out of the couch afterwards. It was pointed out that God is pretty much invisible. 'He'll cover himself in colours for my party,' was the answer. Is he hard to book for private functions? 'Nope. I'll just write a letter and throw it up into the air.'

And she has. 'Dear God, Please come to my ballerina party.'

We're looking forward to this. God in a tutu doing balloon tricks. I must remember the camera.

Mothers' mantra

Are you tired of screaming at the kids like a referee every morning? What you need is a recorded message so that you can whack it on the cassette player and let it rip while you hit the snooze button. All together now:

Will you get out of bed? You'll be late. Did you hear what I said? Get out of bed! You'll miss the bus if you don't get out of bed. What do you want on your sandwiches? Are you in the shower yet? I'm not driving you to school. If you miss the bus you can bloody well walk. What do you want on your sandwiches? I don't know where your socks are I told you to lay them out last night! Vegemite, peanut butter, jam . . . Are you in the shower? Well get OUT OF BED and get in here and have some breakfast. You ARE having breakfast you're NOT going to school on an empty stomach. You are not sick. You are not staying home. I don't know where your bag is I gave it to you last night. Don't forget your sports gear and your jumper. They're probably with your socks. I don't know where your socks are. Can I have a bit of support here?

'Do what your mother says.'

You've got three minutes to catch the bus.

When you're ready, you can tackle other family classics such as No I'm not going to give you any more money *and* Go ask your father, *not to mention* Are you deaf? You'll eat what you're given *and the old favourite* What are you doing in there?

Fantasy Island

It was Robert Benchley, the famous American parent, who said: 'There are two classes of travel. First class and with children.' Parents quote him to one another as they stand, hand in hand, watching a tropical sunset over a blue lagoon for one-eighth of a second, until smaller hands tug at their sarongs and tell them Jason just stood on a snake and he's turning blue and Ramone just drank water from the tap and can't leave the bathroom and why doesn't paradise have a better range of videos? It happens to all parents. It's as much of a shock as the cost of the first school shoes.

Your husband says to you, 'Let's have a lovely weekend away. Somewhere really nice. Let's pamper ourselves.' Oh yes! You see a table for two on the veranda, palms, moonlight on the sea, you and your husband talking. To each other! Plans for the future! Plans like throwing in the jobs and living on a coral island. We could home-teach the kids. The kids! Oh yes. They're the ones under the next table, looking up the sarongs or weeping for a toy left at home.

But beware the 'family' destinations. There's one off the coast of Queensland. Their water supply is exclusively imported. From Bangladesh after the wet season. Local fishermen reel in the viruses, bigger than barramundi. An all-night romp with your husband is when your four-year-old is up all night vomiting after swallowing half the pool. You call the resident doctor, whose eyes look like two Bloody Marys, and who diagnoses the water and assures you he never drinks it. He prescribes rum and antibiotics with a little umbrella on top.

Where is the You Wish family resort? You get off the plane. Masseurs fall on you and your husband, and carry you to your bar stools, kneading vigorously. Strangers take your children. But they're not social workers. They aren't even disguised as fairies or Batman.

They're perfectly disguised as you. Rubber masks. Firmer thighs. More patience. A nicer you. An 'ice-cream and jelly on demand' you. You drink and swim and say, 'Up a bit and more to the right,' to your masseur and spouse where appropriate. The kids? Who knows? At check-out you smoothly replace your impersonators. The kids are polite, tanned, speak Italian, eat broccoli without complaint. Now for a holiday where someone takes away the husband for the same treatment.

Home for the holidays

The last week of the school holidays. For mothers who haven't been able to frolic in the snow or splash through tropical lagoons with the family, or dump the kids on grandma's doorstep in a basket and run, it's the last, longest week. Home alone, with the kids. What to do with the darlings? If it's going to the movies or the theatre, read the advertisement carefully. Don't just go by the title. *Eraser* is not a heart-warming story of animated classroom stationery. *Little Shop of Horrors* is not the stage version of Toys 'R' Us. (That's called *Shop of Little Horrors*.) I want you to avoid my parents' trauma when they accidentally took us kids to see the film *Barbarella*. We were all under the age of nine. Who knows why they thought this was a children's film? Perhaps they thought it was an animated family classic. Barbie meets Cinderella.

The opening scene was Jane Fonda floating around a space capsule, stripped down to her fur bikini, and I mean that literally. By the time Barbarella was strapped into the machine which was supposed to pleasure her into submission (but which she overcame, if you know what I mean) my parents were horrified and wanted to leave. We, of course, wanted to stay and the threat of a triple tantrum was more of a health risk than odd looks from the locals in those days. Nowadays, if you accidentally took your children in to an R-rated film, social workers would confiscate your children. (They will certainly take your children if you have a fag in the foyer afterwards.) Having social workers take your children would be helpful the first week of the holidays but it's a bloody nuisance in the last week.

Barbarella caused no lasting damage, although Jane Fonda's aerobics tapes still make me think about a high rise wax job. And for years I thought that an orgasm automatically gave you a new hairdo. Which actually led to good sex as it was a strong incentive to direct partners to the hot roller button.

Stick to simple film titles. *The Hunchback of Notre Dame* says it all. Deformity and persecution in medieval France. Kids love it and there are hundreds of dollars worth of Hunchback toys to argue over. The only merchandise from *Barbarella* was inflatable and I think my brother hid it in the garden shed.

The last laugh

A bunch of experts has cobbled up a survey claiming that children laugh up to 400 times a day, but adults only laugh an average of eleven times a day. Well, where do adults lose 389 of the laughs they had in childhood? Easy. Twenty laughs go when you meet green food and know you'll have to eat it. Thirty laughs evaporate when you realised that your first day at school is not your only day at school. Just the beginning of sixteen long years. Twenty laughs vamoose when you discover you're short/tall/fat/thin with big feet/big breasts/no breasts, have thin hair/curly hair/straight hair, or just one nostril bigger than the other. And as for adolescence . . . well, Romeo and Juliet didn't die laughing.

Come puberty and that first period – and thirty more years of them – fifty laughs flush away. The first sexual encounter. Fuuttt! Thirty laughs gone in sixty seconds. And another thirty when you realise that one day you'll have to do it sober. Thirty more chuckles elope the day you walk down the aisle thinking, 'Oh well, there's always divorce.' Prenatal classes? 'That head goes through this hole?' Minus twenty. (Nervous laughter doesn't count.) The last thirty laughs disappear when your breasts develop their own laugh lines.

Is it fair? I've decided kids have all the laughs because what they mainly laugh at is adults. And it is fair. We did, too.

Feeding Frenzy

Food Nazis

Stop! Put down the fruit juice crammed full of vitamins, minerals and trace elements of fruit. For years, nutritionists have told us that fruit juice is so damn healthy it should be sold on prescription. That the only thing healthier than fruit juice was going to the hot springs at Lourdes and lowering a bucket. Not this week.

Nutritionists have just announced that fruit juice is bad for us. We would be better off drinking milk. Yes, milk. The same stuff that nutritionists used to tell us would turn our arteries into Milky Way bars. Well, I'm sorry, but go tell that to the crew of *Endeavour*. 'No lime juice for me today thanks, Captain, I'll just have a malted milk.' You'd get a free set of lashes and I don't mean Cutex.

Do not panic. Remember when potatoes were the enemy? Red meat? Red wine? Then they discovered that red wine tidies up the cholesterol from red meat which we need for iron anyway, and we had a balanced diet all the time.

Next week, the nutritionists will tell us that fruit juice cures shingles, pancreatitis and death. They might even find that it prevents scurvy and we'll be back to 1770, on the good ship *Endeavour*, keeping an eye out for a galleon flying the Mr Juicy flag.

This is because nutritionists are the quacks of food. Although that's an insult to ducks and I love ducks . . . especially cooked in brandy and cream with orange sauce. The only food they agree on is beans. Nutritionists thrive on a crisis.

They're like soldiers who start wars. They're like memory recovery therapists who tell you your dad whacked you because he was a Satanist, not because you put Clag in the lawnmower. They are like firefighters who become arsonists: lighting little fires at the back of buildings, then screaming, 'Evacuate!' (Daily please and preferably after breakfast.)

Nutritionists are ratbags. In fact, there are only three rules you have to remember about food.

1. Never eat dog liver stew in Burma.

2. When live food is brought to your table for your approval, don't look into its pleading little eyes and give it a name.

3. Beans really are very good for you. Chocolate and coffee both start out as beans.

The plot thickens

I read in the paper that if we don't eat fat we can get very sick because fat activates antioxidants that fight cancer and serious stuff like that. Then on the news a couple of days later a doctor was saying if you over-exercise you will die earlier. See the link? These are both things that nutritionist Nazis and health freaks have been constantly nagging us about for years. Don't eat fat! Exercise!

Too much fat will kill you, so will too much salt and too much sugar. Well of course too much salt and sugar and fat will kill you, that's what too much means! Too much spinach will kill you too as they are now discovering. Too much health food is starving out littlies, stunting their development. Too much exercise leads to early death. Too much means *too much*.

Now that I've found out that fat is good for you and exercise can be bad for you I realise I'm in pretty good shape.

I think we've lost the plot quite frankly. Australia has the best fresh meat, fruit and vegies in the world and we're constantly told not to eat them. Who tells us? Nutritionists! Who encourages us to eat substitute fat, substitute sugar, substitute meat? Nutritionists! Who makes billions of dollars producing substitutes because we're so often told by nutritionists they're better than real food? Multinational food conglomerates. And who are nutritionists sponsored by? Multinational food conglomerates. Mmmm, I feel a conspiracy coming on. Makes me feel like a big cup of coffee with full cream milk and three sugars.

Dear Doctor Jean,

   What are the risks of becoming a vegetarian?

                                        Damien, Perth, WA

Damien, the main risk for people who become vegetarians is that you'll keep bringing it into the conversation at all times, except the one time it might be useful. Such as you've just sat down at a dinner party and the hostess brings in a superb veal casserole she's spent all day on, and you don't tell her you are a veggie until it's served. Even then you won't have to eat it, but you might end up wearing it.

Dear Doctor Jean,

   How do I know if I have halitosis?

                                        Melody, Mildura, Vic

Melody, you know you have halitosis when your friends suggest you suck on something to sweeten your breath, and hand you a pair of old football socks.

Dear Doctor Jean,

   What is hayfever?

                                        Clarissa, Guildford, NSW

Clarissa, hayfever is one of nature's wonderful little alibis. Whenever you're stuck for someone's name, or you're backed into a corner by a golfer, just erupt. Spray nasally, uncontrollably, until the moment has passed and say brightly, 'Hayfever.' A spring of privet in the buttonhole can be extremely helpful.

Big Mother is watching us

Let's hear it for the year's silliest public awareness campaign. The Food Safety Campaign. Another hysterical campaign to prove that Australians are victims in their own kitchens. That we can't make a sandwich without counselling. Man leaves ham out of fridge, eighty years later he dies.

Remember the shock footage of a cat licking the butter? Cats like everything! Dogs lick faces. Your husband might kiss you while you're buttering Saos. Do these boneheads know what *happens* to a school lunch after it leaves the school bag? Or what lurks between the health food bar and the salad in the office? Air. Air that is full of germs and dust and aftershave and farts. Do these twinks eat in a surgically sterilised operating theatre?

Have these wusses never been to a barbecue? There isn't a person in Australia on solids who hasn't eaten something that the blowflies haven't picked at first. Or sandflies. Or adventurous mosquitoes. Who hasn't dropped something at a barbecue, picked it up, wiped it on their clothes, a cloth, the dog, and slapped a bit of sauce on it? And yet we survive.

Hormones in pigs make you sick. Antibiotics in chickens make you sick. Irradiated and gassed and frozen vegetables are in our crisper now. They should have kept the camera on the cat after he licked the butter to see if the butter killed him.

Yes, Big Mother is watching us. Although this nine million dollar campaign didn't make a scrap of difference.

After ten years of anti-smoking campaigns, the number of men smoking has fallen by one per cent, the number of women by half a per cent and the number of smoking teenagers is booming. Exercise campaigns? The number of fat men is up five percent and women by three per cent and the number of people who scoff at joggers and take no exercise at all is up five per cent.

Health scare campaigns don't work because we are grown-ups. We know they just make work for fuss bottoms, wowsers and creative directors. And the only words we remember are the naughty ones. Campaigns against fats and cigarettes might as well be campaigns for fats and cigarettes.

The same thing happened in France, incidentally, when French health nags banned booze advertising and the whole country promptly went out and got drunk. Although how anyone could tell beats me. By my estimate the cost to the community of these useless health campaigns is at least fifty billion dollars. Of course I'll need a lot of government money to verify this guess. Some of which I will use to waddle off to lunch.

Dear Doctor Jean,
What is lactose intolerance?

Anna, Gympie, Qld

Anna, lactose intolerance affects people who get impatient with cows, because they're so bloody calm all the time.

Fish farts

I'm not a fan of smoking. The cost to the community is billions of dollars a year for replacing car-seat covers. Sure I smoked when I was fourteen to impress guys who would teach me French kissing. But after twenty years I thought, 'They must be impressed by now, especially the ones with burnt tongues.' And I stopped. But some of the anti-smoking nags are worse than nutritionists.

Take the recent story about pollution. The scariest comparison the excitable experts could make is that pollution's so bad, it's like smoking ten cigarettes a day. Hah! To a proper smoker, ten cigarettes is almost giving up smoking. It's what you smoke over breakfast. It's a warm-up exercise. Ten cigarettes is nothing compared with smoking outside the office when just one car goes by. Say you've got a six-cylinder car and each cylinder has the capacity of a pair of lungs and each cylinder is doing 5,000 revs a minute. Nip down to the shops and back. By the time you get home, your car has pumped out more noxious gases than five football commentators on forty fags a day over ten years.

That's why people who get so anxious about pollution that they want to do themselves in seal the car windows and run a hose off the exhaust. They don't seal the windows and smoke ten Dunhills. All they'd get would be a strong desire for coffee and new car-seat covers.

But is pollution all the fault of cars? Maybe not. I think the main causes of smog these days are:

1. Chargrilled octopus: all those bistros pouring out millions of tonnes of marinated octopus soot.

2. Flaming sambucas after the octopus: An aromatic coffee smog giving the whole atmosphere a monster hangover.

3. Personal trainers who force flubbery clients to burn that lard off: where does the smouldering cellulite go? Up!

4. Maybe fish are the big polluters? Or, to be extremely specific, fish farts? Why not? Backfiring New Zealand sheep knocked that hole in the ozone layer. Billions of fish all munching on smaller fish and blowing off zillions of tiny bubbles, bursting on the surface, forming a great yellow cloud of plankton gas while everybody blames the poor Mazdas. It's a good theory and I'm willing to accept a lot of government money to prove it.

Dear Doctor Jean,

I have recently developed an allergy to balsamic vinegar which means I can't go out to really nice restaurants. Must I stay at home?

Carol, Devonport, Tas

No, Carol. Simply coat your tongue and lips with a sturdy layer of moisture-resistant zinc cream. Preferably the pink one. The yellow or blue could lead to fellow guests forcing mouth-to-mouth resuscitation over the entrees.

Mmm ... pethidine

Ever since humans noticed that walking on the hands and skinning their knuckles was more painful than standing up and pulling a hamstring, good old Homo Erectus has been evolving in response to pain. We all know what we discovered when we rubbed two sticks together. That's right, the blister. This inspired the Bic lighter and the Vulcan oil heater. Doing in our insteps and our backs on rocks led respectively to the wheel and the waterbed. And, after turning one too many limbs into dinner in the microwave, we invented the safety switch.

Pain is the inspiration for human progress, and medical science has done much to help progress along. (See blood tests, internal examinations, enemas, all dental work and people who prod you to see if it hurts.)

So why is medical science now trying to hold back our mighty species by developing pain-killers? Pain-killers are dangerous! They kill pain. Have they no shame? No ethics? Do they want us to regress?

During a recent rest in hospital, I saw suffering of such magnitude – of such horror – that the images haunt me. So let's not talk about the mealtimes. Let's move on to pain. There were women in my ward who cried out in agony, who groaned and moaned in deep distress. Where was the pain relief? My earplugs. But these women were pioneers. 'I only took pain-killers when I swallowed my tongue and my ears fell off,' they skited. Because they knew that if they suffered enough pain science would one day give their body a series of zips, just to make them shut up.

And I blew it. Possibly for all of us. I had pethidine.

'Mmmmmm . . . pethidine,' as Homer Simpson would say if he was allowed to use it at six o'clock on week nights. (In my view, pethidine for all parents at six o'clock on week nights should be compulsory.)

Wonderful, luxurious pethidine. Why bother with holidays? Why can't we just take pethidine for a week? No lost baggage, no roach-happy accommodation, no kids in the car throwing up.

Mmmmmmmm . . . pain-killers are the most ingenious, important, wonderful, super-duper, floaty woaty . . . Can't feel a thing, oh life is wonderful. ISN'T LIFE LOVELY! Ha ha ha. Cut my leg off? Why not, eh? One less sock to pull up . . . Ha ha hah! I'll just walk on all threes. Skinned knuckles? Who cares? Drift. Swoon.

The people who want us to have a new worry every day now want us to put blockout on our cats and dogs. Have these people ever tried to even wash a cat or dog? Have they tried to get sun blockout on a human child? No, our pets do not need sun blockout! As keen students of cats and dogs will tell you when it gets very, very hot they don't try to tan their pink parts. They lick them and lie down. They've enough brains to get out of the sun and lie there panting. They don't even get sponsors and whack away at tennis balls in sixty degree heat. They won't even chase tennis balls. It's only humans who go barking mad under the sun and set up organisations to invent new worries. Next week's worry: why are so many sports officials chasing cars?

And today's dodgy statistic comes from the usual medical experts who make up an epidemic and claim the cost to the community is forty-five billion dollars, and then ask for money.

They've come up with a beauty: it's social phobia. People who don't like to meet other people. People who never leave the house. And the experts say solemnly that this phobia affects one million Australians. How do they know if the buggers never leave the house? You can't do a survey. They wouldn't answer the door!

It's the people who always run into people who don't like to meet people that I feel sorry for. And I'm prepared to feel sorry professionally. Send forty-five billion dollars now.

Superman and the shoe shop

It is statistically true that almost all scientific research exists to fill out the Sunday papers. Otherwise they'd be nothing more than sports results with a comic section. One great piece of medical research revealed that X-rays can be bad for us! What a surprise! *Quelle surprise!* Knock me over and fracture my collar bone with a feather! I thought radiographers wore lead aprons to stop the fat splashing on their shirts! I though they wore lead aprons because they cooked heavy meals. I though they left you with the X-ray machine because of some problem with your body odour. I thought they went into another room behind a three-foot thick wall because they wanted a bit of time alone. I always wondered why they didn't join you and say, 'Mind if I have a couple of snaps taken with you for the family album?'

Of course too many X-rays are bad for us. Why else would you bother with security guards at airports running a dust buster over us to see if we beep. It would be so much easier just to lie on your side with your hand luggage on the conveyor belt and go through the X-ray machine.

I was first swept up by the mystery and romance of X-rays in childhood, when my parents ran a shoe shop. High-tech footwear specialists in those days had do-it-yourself X-ray machines, a sort of guess-your-shoe-size contraption; you inserted your feet and peered through an eyepiece and you could see your bones wiggle.

The idea was to take the guesswork out of finding a pair of shoes that fit, but for kids there is nothing so creepy and thrilling as a glimpse of your own skeleton doing a soft shoe shuffle. It was such an unusual view of yourself, like looking at your own bottom without a mirror, or admiring the back of your own neck.

Of course, it wasn't our only exposure to X-rays. Superman's X-ray vision was undoubtedly the most exotic of his powers. He was strong, but anyone could be strong and since we were children we all believed we were more or less invulnerable. Many of us also believed we could fly. Off garage roofs, for example. And shortly after flying off garage roofs we were initiated into the practical use of X-rays, and learned about the limitations of the plummeting human collarbone, when it collided with the family turning circle.

We never worried about the technical improbabilities of Superman's piercing stare. Such as why he was so selective. He could spot a heroine dangling over a pit full of cobras through a double brick wall, for example, but never peeked through her underwear.

Because his X-rays were in the service of good against evil, that was why.

Of course there was a hint that if X-rays fell into the wrong hands they could be a threat to world peace. The boys of our age used to write away to the sleazy novelty companies which advertised in Superman comics for a pair of genuine X-ray spectacles whose sole function was to see through our underwear. They didn't work, oddly enough, and the little pimples used to blow a month's pocket money finding this out. The spectacles also gave these pocket lechers a permanent squint. Further evidence that X-rays, used correctly, are in the service of goodness.

Dear Doctor Jean,

I think I may have accidentally swallowed the family dog. What should I do?

Robert, Heathwood, Qld

Robert, try to coax him out. Keep some of his favourite toys in your mouth. Or possibly become intimate with the postman.

Dear Doctor Jean,

Recently I developed a rare orange skin rash that no-one could identify, but the specialist told me to do nothing because it would clear up and he wouldn't even charge me. What should I do?

Deborah, Gordon, NSW

Run for it. The man is an imposter. A real specialist would have taken one look at your rash and planned extensions for his house.

Dear Doctor Jean,

What can I do about medical specialists who overload their appointments, and keep me waiting for hours, forgetting that I'm sick, which is why I'm there?

Madelaine, Kerang, Vic

Madelaine, many people pay their specialists three months late, just to let them know how it feels. But for quick service on the day, take a brick in your handbag. If you're kept waiting, lean over reception and threaten to damage the till.

Thanks for the mammaries

The campaign to encourage women to have regular breast examinations has been very successful. My only quibble has been the regular use of the term 'breast awareness' which seems to assume women don't have it. As if we wake up every morning and exclaim, 'Holy cow! Where did *they* come from?'

In truth, if women don't give themselves regular breast checks it isn't because we're careless, but for fear of what we might find. That's why I always examine my breasts lying down. That way, if I do find a lump and I faint, I haven't got far to fall. It's for the same reason that men shirk having prostate tests standing up.

Another reason is that official breast examinations – sticking your breasts between two metal plates and having them crushed like toasting sandwiches – are unpleasant and painful. Or as doctors would say, 'You may experience some discomfort.' Never buy shoes from a doctor.

In contrast, all that blokes have to do is find someone who will stick a couple of fingers up their bums. Not a problem (at least in Sydney) and not much of a deterrent.

But to all the experts who may be concerned about women's breast awareness, don't worry. For much of our lives we've got lots of it. Ask any female teenager.

I couldn't wait to get breasts. But they could. For years, I longed for breasts as least the same size as my knees. My shoulder blades were bigger than my breasts. When I wore my boob tube it looked like my legs were on backwards. The boys didn't just call me flat-chested. They called me concave. I felt like a sexless mutant. At night I'd lie in bed and pull where they ought to be, to make them bigger. Just like boys were doing elsewhere and, I later found out, with equal success.

Even at twenty I was still a double A cup. Which isn't really a bra at all, it's just a couple of yachting flags with a backstrap. But you can't get to twenty and not wear a bra! Boyfriends who didn't have card tricks had to have something to do with their hands.

Suddenly, at twenty-one, my breasts started to grow. I don't know whether it was hormones, sex or vodka. But they grew and grew and grew. At first I thought, 'You beauty, B cups!' Then it was C cups and I thought, 'Oh well, if I must.' But before I knew it I had bazoongas. Two, bigger than my head, DD cups. I had to dig holes in the sand before I could lie on my towel. Bank tellers started to do transactions with my breasts.

I personally slowed down the redevelopment of Melbourne just by walking past building sites, leading to thousands of lost working days in whistling and rude remarks. For years if anyone asked my occupation I'd say 'blushing'.

I spent ten years trying to cover my breasts up. Breasts that had a life of their own. You walk, they trot. You stop, they take another step or two. Breasts that were impossible to dress. No sexy bras for big-busted women. Ask for something flimsy and French in a DD and they look at you as if to say, 'Have you tried Manchester?'

The only thing I never worried about was an extra unwanted lump. But then I went backpacking with a girl-friend for a couple of years, as Aussies do, and she told me about lumps! And breast cancer and breast examinations.

Well, I looked and I found one. In Morocco. I went to the local public hospital. If you've ever seen *Gone With The Wind*, you might remember the Atlanta railway yards full of the wounded. That was the waiting room.

Inside there were dozens of tables covered in blood, and patients everywhere covered in blood, and doctors and nurses covered in blood. I got prodded and pinched and poked and squeezed and they said they'd cut it out straight away but I think they meant cut it off. I said I'd think about it and left.

Two days later I lay on the top of a long tin table with a little padded bit for my head and my left breast in the hands of an old Moroccan doctor and his even older uncle who was helping out as a nurse. Neither spoke English. The walls were cracked and mouldy, one window was broken, and the light bulb hanging over the table was covered with fly spots. I felt the jabs and heard the slice of the knife, the same sound as cutting liver for the cat. My breast lay peeled like a pomegranate. It was about this time that the old nurse sneezed.

The old Moroccan doctor turned out to have a steady hand, in spite of the lousy local funding, and I've still got the full set, and he still has my gratitude. But like the spare socks and the map and the phrase book, it's still something I wished I'd checked before I left.

Flexing Off

Only 365 days till next Christmas

Don't panic! I know most of you are caught in the glare of Christmas lights like a rabbit transfixed by an oncoming semi covered in tinsel. You, too, stand at counters with a fixed smile saying 'Have a Happy Christmas yourself. Can he return this after Christmas? Even with oil on it?'

Meanwhile, we're all thinking: 'I've flashed my purse more often than Sharon Stone.' I want to fling my money in the air and scream. 'Take it, take it all. Just give me something for a bloke who's got everything including novelty boxer shorts because that's what I gave him last year.' Then break down sobbing into Santa's beard.

That sums up Christmas for me. Money slipping through your fingers like those $60 silk shorts he never wore. I would have got Daffy Duck but they only had Porky Pig in his size. I forgot that he was sensitive about his stutter. And so we utter those immortal words, 'Next year I'm not going to leave everything to the last minute.'

Next year I'll be one of those organised people who shops for next Christmas at the January sales. As if I could become one of those people who do their shopping in a calm, disciplined way all year or, even better, hit the January sales and wrap everything by February. Those people must have friendships that last a lot longer than mine. And men who don't change diameter.

I always leave it till the last minute. But with a difference. I'm not your normal idiot. I have method in my idiocy. I think to myself: 'It is the last minute, you're an idiot, don't battle the madding crowd expecting something to take your fancy. It doesn't happen in bars. Why would it in department stores? Plan.' So I make a list. Husbands will get a travelling toiletry set. Perfect. And Dad will get the olive pipper. Yes. Simple. Or so you'd think. But it's not. It's a nightmare. Do you know that nobody sells men's toiletry kits that I like? Toothbrush, shaver, comb, container for soap. Nose hair curlers. Ear wax syringe. Rhino horn tongue suppressant. The basics. Is this too much to ask?

I scour all day for this one present. Then I panic on Christmas Eve and I buy Elmer Fudd boxers. Forgetting his speech impediment. I do find the olive pipper, though. And Dad's got one already. Bought it at the January sales.

If you want to surprise relatives you don't see often, for a very good reason, try this variation on the stuffing. Stuff the turkey with a chicken. Stuff the chicken with a spatchcock. Stuff the spatchcock with a quail and . . . the *pièce de résistance* . . . stuff the quail with a single glass eye. The look on Uncle Frank's purple face will be something the kids remember for ages.

Very disappointed with the crackers this year. They didn't have a paper hat inside! All crackers come with a paper hat. It's as necessary as those reassuring jokes which have entertained you since you were ten.

'Why does a golfer need two pairs of trousers?'

'In case he gets a hole in one!' Answers the whole table, like a wacky sort of grace.

But no hat? What's Christmas to a kid without a scarlet-faced grandparent under a floppy yellow crêpe crown?

This year no-one looked like a complete dork. Well, that's not quite true, but it was entirely the fault of the brandy butter.

No hat. And when you pulled the cracker the only thing that went pop was Uncle Bert's hernia.

Stuff this

The first sign of Christmas isn't the cotton wool on strings in David Jones and the heat-exhaustion epidemic in Santa's Winter Palace. The first sign of Christmas is some smug twit whining in some newspaper about our traditional Christmas dinner.

'Why do Australians, with Christmas in the middle of summer, eat roast turkey, baked potatoes, plum pudding and buckets of brandy butter and cream?' they priss. 'Where's our national pride? Why aren't Australians eating Thai, or Italian, or Tex-Mex Turkish?'

Then they rabbit on about seafoods and salads, and brandish recipes for Lobster with Jim-Jam Dressing and salads of artichoke hearts stuffed with zucchini flowers stuffed with wattle pollen, in a drizzle of A Virgin Once Again olive oil. Followed by Okra Flambé with Jackfruit Conserve and a little umbrella on top.

Why, year after year, do these morons claim Australians are morons for not buying seafood? To buy seafood at Christmas time you need a second mortgage. Prawns for example, go from $12 a kilo to about $240 a kilo. That's because most Australian prawns and lobsters go away for the holidays. To Japan. The weedy remaining lobsters, at $550 a kilo – most of them shell – wouldn't feed a super-model, much less teenagers who've been fasting for a week, in training.

These foodie prigs must also eat out a lot. Try assembling one of their fiddly menus. The only okras round our house at Christmas are the ones in thongs and, as for jackfruit, I presume they're talking about my unfortunate uncle. (Jack only takes his clothes off because he's allergic to the artificial sweetener in cooking sherry.)

Imagine the preparation:

1. Find heart in artichoke and de-vein.

2. Hollow out pine nuts.

3. Stuff artichoke in pine nut.

The only thing that gets stuffed round our place is the turkey and possibly the Bing Crosby *White Christmas* CD. Next peel three bags of spuds and bung them in the oven with a turkey. It's easy, it's quick, and you can do it drunk and get on with Christmassy things like separating the relatives.

But maybe the food snobs are right? In fact, why give kids presents at Christmas? You can do it any time. Bah, humbug. We eat our simple and delicious Christmas dinner because it's Christmas, and because of the association this food evokes. Of which the main association is Christmas, when we were kids, eating inappropriate food and loving it.

Dear Doctor Jean,

What do you say in a note to your hostess after a party during which you raced off her husband?

Pam, Black Rock, SA

Just ask for the recipe of the punch. Also remember you only send a thank you note if you want to be asked back again. Perhaps you could simply send flowers. Along with any of her husband's underwear you may have souvenired. It may have been a gift, with sentimental value.

Dear Doctor Jean,

What do you do when you go to a friend's place for dinner and the hosts love experimenting and the food is dreadful?

Jennifer, Subiaco, WA

Eat it, Jennifer, while plotting your revenge. The next time one of your hosts is sick and helpless, rush around a special soup from your mother's recipe made of equal parts eggplant and anchovies. Spoon it in personally.

Dear Doctor Jean,

How do you handle a guest at dinner who says, 'This is marvellous? What do you put in it?'

Gwen, Bellevue Hill, NSW

If your guest is eating fish fingers and mash at the time, you're probably being insulted. But if you've slaved all day, or even picked up something from the deli, the best approach is to make the recipe up and make it complicated. Throw in tips like, 'It's most important to grow your own cumin,' or 'Don't forget to braise the fennel before you poach the anchovies.' This way your guest will try it at home, make a terrible mess and you'll look even more skilful.

Perfect manners in an imperfect world

Negotiating a social life is more than just dancing backwards while you apologise to others when they tread on your feet. It's learning from your social slips so that you can recognise them when you do them again next time. The following is the *savoir faire* I've learnt from a life of *faux pas*.

Dinner parties are particularly tricky. A persistent problem is the person at a dinner party who insists on talking politics and ramming her opinions down everyone's throat. The best way to deal with this is to agree with her. Agree with her and go one up. Insist that everyone who disagrees with her ought to be shot. Demand a dictatorship to enforce her opinions. Offer to shoot them yourself. She'll feel like someone trying to kick in an open door. And next time you have to invite her, sit her next to someone who passionately believes in aliens.

The more emotional the dinner party the more problems you have. But with luck the guests are so emotional nobody remembers what happened. A real nuisance is the guest who gets really pissed and keeps playing his favourite country and western CD over and over again, thinking it affects everyone. There is only one way to stop him. Sing along with it one word behind.

Then there's the problem of a reckless guest wanting to drive home. How do you get the car keys away from them, politely? Well, you can offer to open the car door yourself and snap the key off. This is a good ploy unless you don't want them to stay the night. Another tactic is to slip your own car key onto your friend's key ring during the evening. He or she will sit there fumbling with it until dawn or until they burst into tears. But the best ploy is to save one moist dessert and slip it onto the driver's seat before departure. No matter how fuelled your friend is, male or female, no-one can roar away with cold blancmange bottom.

Dear Doctor Jean,

I can never remember people's names at parties. What can I do?

Natalie, Gosford, NSW

Remembering names is a common problem with any party. Most of us just keep on chatting to the anonymous guest in the hope that he or she will, for no apparent reason, drop their full name into a sentence. This increases the risk that you will have to introduce them to someone else. It's very tempting to blurt out, 'You can't have been very interesting last time. Who the hell are you?'

But a direct approach may be mistaken for rudeness. The polite tactic is to texta a large scar just under your hairline. At the right moment, you display this and say, 'I'm sorry, but since the operation, I can't remember names.'

Alternatively, when someone whose name you don't know approaches you, just stagger a little, grab their upper clothing, put your name right into the ear and say, 'Try the punch. It's dynamite.'

Don't forget to slur. If you can, throw up on their shoes, it will look really authentic. No-one will care if you can't remember them. In fact, they'll prefer it.

The arts end of the world

What is it with the Sydney Festival – or any festival for that matter? Every year the usual suspects roll up. Misery-guts Irish theatre troupes complaining about the price of potatoes. Bitter little feminist masterpieces from the UK. Dance troupes in ethnic frocks from everywhere else, sponsored by Benson and Hedges and grizzling about capitalism. Italian operas full of bursting bodices and broken hearts. The whole bunch of them needs whinge counselling. And they always turn up in Sydney during the summer holidays when the beaches are packed, the waves are sparkling, and the nights are warm and full of stars and barbecues.

The best thing about living in Sydney during the festival is that most people don't even know it's on. And if you told them, they'd put another squirt of factor fifteen in the marinade, whack another steak on, and turn up the soundtrack from *South Pacific*.

Sometime during the Sydney Festival there's Opera in the Park where tens of thousands of people pack out a local paddock for a singalong. But that's not the Arts, thank God. That's a party.

Australia does have Artists, like it or not. We also have flashers and vegetarians and the gun lobby. And let it fairly be said, Australian artists are as miserable as any artists in the world. World class gripers. What they don't have is the nation's attention. The only people who read Australian novels are Australian novelists. Who goes to Australian plays? Enemies of the playwright – usually other playwrights. And who buys Australian paintings? Insurance companies with empty wall space in their palaces, who buy them by the square metre.

Sometimes our Artists produce actual works of Art, which we celebrate. We celebrate by gathering at the airport to wave them off, overseas. When they get overseas, of course, they discover why people who emigrate to Australia don't go back. Because the Arts overseas are rotten with seriously depressed foreign intellectuals, flogging fads like deconstructionism and post-modernism. Wayward worms who aim to turn the Arts to compost. This makes our Artists even more miserable, but as our leading Arts patron said recently, 'So what?' We're not going to fly them back.'

Because we all know what it is about Australia that encourages people from so many distant lands to pack themselves into frail, rickety fishing boats, or hide in the hold of foreign aircraft, or even marry our politicians, in the desperate hope of getting to Australia and being allowed to stay.

It's not our freedom from arrogant and despotic governments. Nor is it to escape from economic chaos. No way. They'd all be piling into Belgium if that's all they wanted. No, it's a desperate attempt to find a country free of the tyranny of the Arts.

What was it that drove our convict ancestors to commit their harmless crimes – the theft of a handkerchief or farting in church – and then turn themselves in, saying, 'It's a fair cop. Show me to the First Fleet! Rum, buggery and the lash? Sounds like Sydney!'

What was it? They wanted to get away from bloody Gainsborough's gallery openings, pissy chamber music and

Byron poncing about in poetry and getting his lithograph in the papers, that's what.

And why did hundreds of thousands of immigrants suddenly down tools and jump ship for Ballarat? It wasn't gold. It was to get away from people yammering on about Beethoven and *David Copperfield* at dinner parties, and the looming threat of French Impressionism.

Have you ever noticed how the great waves of twentieth century immigration to Australia have coincided with exciting surges in the Arts overseas? Cubism. Look out! Here come the Spaniards. Soviet realism? Make way for the Eastern Europeans. Fellini infects civilisation and half a million Italians head for the airport at interval.

The Snowy River scheme was built by people fleeing the works of Gertrude Stein. Germans came here to get away from Berlin architecture. Now the Chinese are flocking to Australia to escape two thousand years of Chinese opera, bringing with them the secret knowledge of an ancient culture, that Chinese opera sounds like a cat with a cracker up its arse being dragged down a blackboard. And they'd rather find a good karaoke bar.

It is true that some early settlers landed in Sydney and heard about dreams of an Opera House, or fetched up in Adelaide and saw Colonel Light mincing about, laying out surveyor's pegs for a festival centre and wondering what to call the bistro. Undeterred these hardy Philistines loaded their families into bullock wagons and set out for the interior, for that promised land where the Arts would never reach. Where the seeds of blank verse and atonal music would never flourish. A paradise where even the most persistent muse would take one look and say, 'Sod this. I'm going back to Paris!' and let people get on with their lives. And that's where they founded Canberra.

We don't mind. We've got an Oscar for frocks. We don't miss the Arts. We've got entertainment instead. We've got symphonies in the park with a few beers, and television and comedy festivals and David Williamson and ten minutes with a good book. And what's the biggest selling book in Australia ever? Max Walker's cricket anecdotes. It's got pictures. You want community involvement in the Arts? Put ten bucks on an outsider in the Archibald. That's entertainment! Entertainment that makes us feel good, that's life-enhancing. Entertainment in a land where people came because life was better than the Arts in the first place.

Dear Doctor Jean,

What do I do at the cricket when I've filled my beer cups with urine and I'm running out of hands.

Simon, North Sydney, NSW

Simon, why not wait until the final ball of the day and just throw them over the people in front of you. Someone's bound to have won and your drenched new friends might think it's champagne. It works at the Grand Prix.

Feng Shui: the art of making your occasional tables the centre of the universe.

風
水
Tom wonders whether Feng Shui could have given his Australia Day barbie harmony in relation to the bastards who arrived next to him.

Tom, from the Polaroids, I can see you being thumped. You can avoid this by getting there earlier and carefully selecting a site upwind. Then, in your ceremonial barbie, burn some traditional fragrant firelighters. The incense, or metho, will clear a very personal space around you. Next, stake out your territory with objects in the eight energy points – small jade dragons, the Esky, the deckchairs, grandmothers and, of course, the speakers for the very loud music. You can also create an area of personal harmony by drinking the correct number of tinnies. Six is the number of argument; ten is the number of danger; but fifty-eight is the number of happiness. And don't forget to drop the chops. This will bring you closer to living things like grass and ants.

Sand rash

Summer. It's not what it used to be. Once the main danger of summer was the blowflies queuing to get to the barbe-cued snags before you did. Now summer is fraught with more danger than a G-string in a big surf. Will it have the same effect as dental floss? Will it have to be surgically removed? What will this G-string cost the community?

The only people working through the holidays are the experts who estimate the cost to the community of every-thing. I haven't finished my sums on the cost to the community of summer but I imagine it will be at forty-eight billion dollars. Or two hundred billion or something.

Once kiddies all over Australia would wait for the sum-mer sun, rip off all their clothes and plunge under the sprinkler, or throw themselves into the Clarke's pool, or get endlessly dumped in the sea. The most you needed was a pair of Speedos and a rolled-up towel on the head like Lawrence of Arabia. Not anymore. Now the summer sun means it's time to rug up. You have to wear more clothes to go swimming than you do to go shopping. First the neck-to-knee cozzie, then the tinted goggles and then the creams. Kids these days are smothered in more cream than a pavlova. Blow the community, what about the cost to the parents? At least the Factor 90 grease is buoyant. It keeps the little ones afloat. But what about the cost to the community of hand-cleaning molluscs, smothered by anti-UV cream slicks? The last thing a mollusc wants is to be water resistant.

And the sun isn't the only danger. There's also the treacherous shade. For thousands of years we've been sit-ting in the shade. Silly old us. Those killer UV rays get in everywhere. If the falling leaves don't get you first. Then there's the shocking cost to the community of sand rash. Particularly sand rash in your personal shady areas. Sand! The nation's number one menace! Shells up the freckle! Grit up the nose! Belly rash! And what about dropped ice-creams! Wet thighs sticking to car seat covers! The trauma! The stress! The lifelong psychological aversion to vinyl! The cost to the community! At *least* forty-five billion dollars if it's carefully fudged.

The cost to the community of people calculating costs to the community over summer, down in their basements, in their cardies, hunched over their calculators, must be enormous. Especially when the community's off at the beach. They might feel left out, get stressed, take leave. Could the community afford it? Or is the community having too much summer fun to care?

Sydney in summer is disgusting – something you don't read in any damn brochure. The humidity is unendurable; we, the people, are drenched in sweat; nobody can sleep; everything's sticky and listless; and it makes people crabby. We get spongy armpit rage. *Who can we take it out on?*

Now I am very, very careful not to snap at my demanding daughter or my sweaty, listless, lie-around-the-house-panting-and-licking-himself husband. I just take it out on that infuriating Channel Ten weatherman, the self-basting, golden brown, chirpy, grinning midget idiot. Because the clown *loves* this weather. Every night he's grinning like a doofus about how, wow, it's summer at last, yippee!

Perhaps if you're a weatherman you can spend all day at the beach. Come news time, he's always standing somewhere cool with a gentle breeze playing around his teeth. The hell with him! Make him pre-record the weather at three in the morning when he can't sleep like the rest of us. Or when he's cleaning the sauna that the rest of us call home. Get a job, lose that tan, wake up and smell those armpits and show a bit of humanity! There, that feels a little better.

Jargon hunting

Holidays make me flinch. It isn't just the thought of a hus-band's knees in shorts, or the discovery that your swimming costume has apparently shrunk since last year, but only around the bottom. Or the challenge of explain-ing to a child that all her Barbies can't come – they just want a quiet holiday at home tidying up their accessories in her bedroom. With a front end-loader.

The problem is the brochures. Each one offers perfec-tion photographed from behind palm trees, and a pool the size of the Adriatic with only slightly smaller drinks. So how to choose? You only get a few precious weeks a year and it's crucial to choose the right destination.

Even the word 'destination' is daunting. Like you're destined to be there. And if you take packages you are. You've already paid. You're stuck. We all know what the real estate jargon really means. 'Neat as a pin' means it's too small to bend over and pick one up, for example.

And travel brochures also have their own code:

Tropical paradise: Enough humidity for your fingernails to grow mould. Adam and Eve from the next cabin making apple sauce all night in the pool.

Adventure island: A wind-swept rock surrounded by shards of coral so sharp they shred the sharks.

Secluded island miles from care: Miles from the nearest doctor and you'll need one because if the mosquitoes don't carry off your children the water supply will.

Relaxed atmosphere: Takes two hours to find someone to show you to your room.

Enjoy the regional customs: The locals get pissed on something brewed from bananas and kero.

Children's program: A large staff member carries children off to play with rabid monkeys.

Local cuisine: Those aren't edible, are they?

Honeymoon specials: Warm champagne on arrival. The table for two nearest the bar.

Mood lighting: Only one lamp works.

Budget: The room on the ant nest, next door to the island's sewage treatment plant. Twenty minutes walk through the island's sewage treatment swamp to the beach.

Family resort: The rooms are small, concrete and used to be shops the owners couldn't rent. Activities exclude everything but bloody jet-skis. The same as a holiday in a shopping centre during the Bathurst 500.

All facilities free: One tennis racket, one ball, one staff member. One paddle board. No paddle. Lots of bloody awful jet-skis, driven by hoons high on banana and kero.

Unique holiday experience: Once is enough.

Holiday from hell

There are some holidays that are so disastrous they are burned into your memory forever, like a bad tattoo of an old flame. Mine was a family holiday in 1961. I know it was bad because ever since this holiday, whenever the words 'Philip Island' are uttered, our family shudders and falls silent. January 1961. I was six, my sister four and my brother two.

This January we were going to the beach, and we were staying in a beach house. A client of dad's had offered him the use of it for a week. We were terribly excited. Visions of cane furniture on cool verandahs, flickering light on mozzie nets, the sparkling sea at the doorstep, and lots of frolicking in the waves. Fun, fun, fun!

Adding to our excitement, Dad had finally finished rebuilding a 1951 Buick. It was a straight 8 cylinder with a balanced engine and four SU carbies. Dad had taken the roof off. It was painted a lairy red. The car was very flat and very fast and very powerful.

We kids loved it. Mum was a little less excited. For one thing, my brother was a babe in arms and a car without a roof was going to be blowy and hot. For another, it only had two front seats. My sister and I had to sit on the back floor. No seatbelts in those days and in this case no seats. Dad put cushions down for us and we took off.

The first disaster happened to the car. After two hours it caught on fire. Possible from the friction of our bums. Flames burst from under the bolted-on bonnet. When Dad had put in his special, huge carbies he hadn't allowed for the fuel pipe that fed them to droop when it got hot, which it did, right onto the exhaust pipe, which melted a hole in the line. Petrol ran onto the red-hot exhaust and immediately caught fire. The look on dad's face is perhaps something only blokes who've spent two years of family life working on their cars can fully appreciate. Shock is putting it too mildly. It was more the look of a man undergoing unexpected open heart surgery without anaesthetic.

We were there for hours while dad cleaned out the carbies and Mum wished she'd married someone else.

The next thing to happen was typical of Victoria in January, especially in an open-top car. The rain came down and the car filled up. During those times when you think your parents will kill each other there is always something that distracts you. In this case it was the thought of the beach house. Ah, the deep-shadowed verandah and the tropical shutters sending bars of light across the honey-coloured floor-boards.

By the time we arrived it was dark. The beach house was not a house, it was not a cabin, it was not even a shack. It was a dump. It was a home-made, unfinished frame of a shed with no lining on the fibro walls and no ceiling under the roof – only beams on which dozens of birds roosted. There were gaps in the floor (my brother disappeared down one); mice scurried everywhere; and the only bedding was a couple of filthy mattresses. It was horrid and Mum erupted. It had been a long day.

We kids didn't mind staying. Birds inside were fairly rare, after all, and mice scuttling to their holes by torchlight were as novel as fairy penguins.

That night we all slid onto the same mattress to sleep, although we did move it after we found our heads were under the direct firing line of the birds. Tomorrow came, and so did the change in the weather – too awful. Gales blew off the Arctic and straight across the dunes. It was windier inside the house than behind it. My little sister was looking out the back door contemplating the lack of back steps when the wind caught it and flung it open. There she swung above an eight foot drop, clinging to the flywire door. Mum screamed.

Dad took us fishing, so Mum could relax in the hovel, I assume. We caught fish. Heaps of fish, dozens of fish. Mullet. Gritty, oily, muddy mullet. None of us would eat them, of course, but we enjoyed bringing them home to Mum and stuffing them in the kerosene fridge. We left that afternoon. I think Mum left first and we quickly packed and picked her up a mile or so down the road, hitching.

As a surprise gift to our kind benefactor we left all our mullet in his kerosene fridge. We thought he'd be down to his salubrious beach house the following weekend, possibly to put on a roof. Nope. He didn't get down there for a couple of months.

The kero had run out by then of course, and all he found was a festering fridge full of rotting mullet. Apparently he and a mate loaded the fridge onto the back of his ute and dumped it into the ocean to defuse. It's probably still there. This may surprise you, but we've never been back to look.

Men and Women: Why?

Sugar & Spice Girls

We still need more women in business. Especially as managers. When the need arises for a ruthless executive who needs no sleep, with a velvet fist in an iron glove, what they need is a woman. Don't believe the propaganda that women are essential in business because they accentuate the gentle, caring side of business. This is all based on a misunderstanding of chemistry.

The first biology lesson for little girls contains the reassuring information that girls are made of sugar and spice while yucky boys are a roulade of snakes and snails and puppy dogs' tails. Feminists have never improved on this, they just made it sound more scientific. Girls are caring, sharing oestrogen, hurray! Boys are aggressive, missile-fondling, war-mongering, hateful testosterone, boo! But now the jig is up. Now some scientists have discovered that oestrogen is the magic ingredient that causes aggression, not testosterone. Well, der! A quick comparison of Roseanne and Homer Simpson could have told them that. And what do they think PMT is? When your sugar and spice levels hit critical mass?

In fact, why didn't they just have a quick look at history? There have been about seven billion women in the world since people began. And they have all had periods twelve times a year for say thirty years; that's about two and a half trillion periods. That's right, approximately five trillion days of PMT. Or putting it more simply, the world has endured around fourteen billion years of smashed crockery and ripped up photographs and broken engagements and false accusations and women storming out of the house screaming, 'I hate the way you breathe when you eat!'

Testosterone is a more warm and cuddly sort of hormone. Just look at penises, they're friendly (too bloody friendly some would say), indiscriminately friendly. They just want to be liked, often. They're like those annoying little dogs that jump up at you, sniffing, licking, whimpering. Trouser Jack Russells. Very easy to deal with: just give them a pat, toss them a biscuit and send them outside to bark at passing cars.

Try doing that with a woman charged with oestrogen, and you're likely to find all your clothes out on the street with the crotch cut out of your strides faster than you can say, 'What did I do?'

More women in business means a hyperactive sales pitch that won't take no for an answer. That won't take anything for an answer except, 'Whatever you say.'

Dear Doctor Jean,

Is the brain a muscle or an organ?

Adam, Greenacre, NSW

Fascinating question, Adam. The male brain is an organ on Friday nights, for example. Given enough to drink, it can turn the whole male body into a single organ. But, on Saturday morning, the brain reverts to a ball of muscle.

With the female, the brain is an organ when it wants something. And a muscle when it doesn't get it. The choice is yours.

There was a survey in the newspapers which asked the British what they want most from a beach holiday. British women mostly wanted laughs and British men wanted sex. So the women get the best of it, because if there's one thing funnier than British men with their clothes off on a beach wearing nothing but their socks, it's watching them attempt sex with third degree sunburn.

Australians everywhere were impressed by Mrs Bronwen Bishop's claim that she was 'the first woman to go down on an Australian submarine'. And Australian women everywhere are asking, 'Where did she get the patience?' At least we now know what submarine captains want when they shout: 'Dive! Dive! Dive!'

Grrls grrls grrls

As a woman, what I like most, apart from a Jane Austen revival, is a good feminist conspiracy theory. And the latest femininist conspiracy theory is that computers are deliberately designed by men to baffle women. And it's so true.

I'm just a stupid girl. These computers are just so confusing. I just don't know what to dust first. All those little cracks between the little button thingummies with the stuff written on them, what are they called again? Oh yeah, letters. Well letters are guys' stuff, where's the plug for the hot rollers? And there's nowhere to put a nailpolish bottle. No wonder I'm stressed. How can I have something that sits on my desk that doesn't have a mirror! I have looked for the button that turns your screen into a mirror but, you know, I don't think they have one. Unbelievable!

Men have deliberately designed computers to be female unfriendly. Don't tell me that calling that thing on a string a mouse isn't part of their plan. The first time I saw it I jumped on my chair. 'EEK!' I couldn't go near it until I was completely sure it was dead. And what about the colour of a Mac PowerBook 150? I mean grey? What sort of colour is that? I will believe there is not a plot when they design a computer that comes in Tropical Lush, Passion Surprise or anything else that sets off my skin tone and moisturises at the same time.

And I suppose I'm just sensitive, you know, because I'm a woman, but having a button marked 'Enter' is sheer harassment. They might as well have called it 'Penetrate'. They might as well have a button with a penis on it. Instead of 'Enter' they could have called it 'Immigrate'. A more sort of embracing, caring, travelling kind of image. It means the same thing as 'Enter'. Sort of. I looked it up in the computer's thesaurus – whatever that means.

Computers of the nineties are like cars of the seventies. They're for the boys to talk about, not for girls to drive. I mean I thought Internet was a pantyhose. And it's not the first time. There are lots of machines men have designed to deliberately confuse women. Mobile telephones. Vibrators which are really technical because they have batteries in them. Yeah, they're really difficult. That's why most women end up using them as apple corers.

Dear Doctor Jean,

How do I deal with men who spread their legs wide on bus seats, leaving me no room?

Joan, Broadmeadows, Vic

Joan, the old bottle of port in a brown paper bag trick is still good. Drink out of it messily while swearing to yourself. People tend to get off the bus early. Otherwise, just wait until a bumpy section of the bus route, or one with lots of corners, and start painting your nails with a trembling hand. Nobody likes Flaming Passion knees.

Whither the wrigglies?

There was a very disturbing newspaper article over the Rice Bubbles recently. It revealed that men's sperm count has dropped by half. This isn't a small survey. We're not just talking about a couple of local blokes being polite to the woman with the clipboard and the little Vegemite jars outside Safeways. This is international research. There were women with little jars and clipboards all over the world. Same conclusion. Only half the fish are biting.

And everyone is asking, 'Why?' Except me. I know why. Men are just running out because men nowadays let 'em loose a lot more than they did fifty years ago. There's rampant promiscuity, what with more women willing to say, 'Why not? I'd do anything to get these shoes off.'

And there are more opportunities in cars. Not only are back seats more comfortable if you're in company, but there are more automatics for blokes to have one hand free when they're not. Look at them driving to work. Women know that look of concentration. They're not all listening to Michael Bolton.

I think this is great. Now he'll only doze off straight away half the time. Because I've never understood why men produce so much sperm in the first place. It's a flaw in men's evolution. You only need one wriggly to make a baby and here they are pumping out millions. So perhaps it's just Mother Nature getting efficient. Women have one egg a month and maybe men are slowly beginning to catch up.

After all, ejaculating a crowd scene must make conception a lot less efficient. All those thousands of little extras rushing out of the starting gate, fighting to get the best position on the inside rail. I tell you, it must be chaos. It must be like a car park after a grand final. It must be like Pamplona during the running of the bulls. You can imagine the stampede, the casualties!

Just think how much more efficient the whole process would be if there were only, say, twenty sperm sauntering up the fallopian way. They could stroll in twos. Like a fire drill. When they get to the egg they could just draw straws. So much nicer than the normal pandemonium, which must be like a bomb scare in a London Tube station. And, even better, it leaves only nineteen sperm someone has to sleep on. Rather than nine million. It can't be comfortable for him.

Dear Doctor Jean,

I've just read about something called transient sexual amnesia and I think I've got it. Every time I make love I can never quite remember if it happened or not.

Paul, Katherine, NJ

Paul, this could mean you're a woman.

Sean Connery had the fish

Young women think men have lost the art of chivalry. Of course they have, you dingbats. Why did we slightly more mature women burn our bras? So that men would run to our aid with a bucket of water and a brand-new Lovable? So men could get a better view of our knockers?

No, we burned them to stop men opening doors for us. So they wouldn't be 'doorist'. What are we? Entrance-deficient? Whether I've got two arms full of shopping and a howling pram, or two portable phones and a briefcase, I don't need some patronising bloke to hold open a door saying, 'Allow me.' I'd rather crawl to the door on my hands and knees, and open it with my head than be demeaned like that. Some women now say that we burned our bras to stop giving men an advantage. Later, we found that bras were also for our convenience. They say it's the same as men and doors. That when we burned our bras we burned a few bridges as well. Traitors!

We burned our bras to stop men paying for us at dinner. How humiliating is that? How would you like Sean Connery to flash his Gold Card, and say, 'Allow me?' It would put you right off, wouldn't it? Wouldn't it? I'd feel much more attractive as a person if Sean said, 'Right, I had the soup and the fish, you ate the oysters, the pheasant, the mini-pizzas, the chocolate tartufo and drank most of the champagne. Yours is $258.75.' Who wouldn't?

And we burned our bras so men wouldn't bloody flatter us. Yuk. There's nothing more offensive than Sean saying, 'Nice earrings!' in that skin-tingling accent. How dare he? He'd never say that to a man. And I don't think we have gone far enough. Next time a man offers me his seat on the bus, I'll go for his knackers.

Sisters! Men can be as charming, and as rugged and huggable in a Shetland jumper, and as well-meaning as they like, but I'll be buggered if they're going to open the door for us. Because if we're going to be equal we have to let them go first.

Dear Doctor Jean,

On Fridays after work everyone in the office goes to the local pub for drinks, but I always drink too much. Then I'm all over the guys I work with. 'I love you, let's go home,' that sort of stuff and this is causing problems on the job.

Trish, Wangaratta, Vic

Trish, problems at work aren't caused because your fellow workers see you drunk on Friday night, but because they see you with a hangover the morning after, and they remember this on Monday. Don't ruin your young life. Start acting responsibly! It's time for safe sex. Go drinking with people from another office.

Fitting mirrors to the glass ceiling

A judge says, 'It is not unknown for a woman to sleep her way to the top,' and women's groups fluff their feathers indignantly and say, 'No woman would!' Phew. What a relief. Another slur upon the perfection of women has been sat upon. Cleopatra was not a serial social climber who climbed all over Julius Caesar and Mark Antony and Richard Burton, but a social worker among Romans with a mid-career crisis. Why all the fuss?

Some women have always dealt with the glass ceiling by fitting mirrors to it and stretching out on a bearskin rug. There is a well-known anecdote in which a rich tycoon asked his voluptuous dinner companion, 'Madam, would you sleep with me for a million dollars?'

The woman replied, 'Yes.'

The man furthered, 'Would you sleep with me for ten dollars?'

Woman: 'Of course not. What do you think I am?'

He said: 'We've established what you are. Now we're haggling over price.'

He missed the point. A woman is not a prostitute if sex is a career move. Only if sex is a career. Madam's career might have been remarkably heightened by a million dollar romp. She might have opened a shop.

Some women have risen horizontally and done a terrific job. There's Marilyn Monroe's famous quip on receiving her first Oscar, 'That's the last producer I'll have to "impress"' (she used a slightly more graphic expression). The casting couch is a bed of thorns, but it does exist, and not every actress has said, 'No thanks, I'd rather stay a waitress.' Anyone who denies it must have slept through the last twelve Jackie Collins novels, and Joan Collins's life.

There are women who work hundred-hour weeks to get on, and there are some women who lie back and think of promotion. Either way, there's no job security. If you're a dishwasher who wants to be a chef, whatever technique gets you into the kitchen, eventually you'll have to cook something.

Women used to be more realistic. Mrs Dale Carnegie was Dale Carnegie's secretary. Once hitched, she wrote a book called *How to Help Your Husband Get Ahead*. Part of it is a guide warning women how to deal with hubby's secretary. And let's not be sexist. Some men would also sleep their way to the top, but there aren't enough women at the top to sleep with. Now that is the problem.

Dear Doctor Jean,
My boss is getting married. What should I give him?
Susanna, Glenelg, SA

Respect tradition, Susanna. Leave the baby in a basket outside the honeymoon suite. Then take a screwdriver and leave a raw prawn inside his laptop.

Nice legs – shame about the workplace

Another bloke has just had his career destroyed on the grounds of sexual harassment. Hooray! The sooner we get these lechers out of the workforce the better. He was a doctor, too. He actually, and I hope you're sitting down for this, commented on his female colleague's appearance. Poor woman. You go to all that trouble with your hip-and-thigh diet, hair bounce, lip gloss, skin tone, power dressing, shoes that match your executive briefcase – and what does some bastard do? He tells you that you 'Look nice.' They should have dangled him from the glass ceiling by his prostate, if they could do it without puckering their Armanis.

You can't pull the swab over my eyes. I know what doctors are like. When I was young and sensitive, I once played a bit part as a prostitute on the old *Young Doctors* soapie. I walked on set in a revealing outfit and looked up to discover a close-up of my breasts on all the television monitors. We didn't have harassment then, just occasionally annoying yobs. In the absence of a tribunal, I empowered my left hand and gave them a two finger salute on all forty-eight monitors. Then I went home and got suppressed-anger counselling from a $10 bottle of wine.

Mind you, it's just as well we didn't have harassment. All those coarse cries of 'Nice legs'. I could have been in court, my feminist credentials in tatters. Flimsy tatters, with a low back and the occasional sequin. Well, he did have nice legs. I don't know how we survived the harassment in some studios. Well, I do. 'Nice legs!' led to 'Love the blouse!' and other outrages (whisky, lunch, jewellery, physical contact in cramped working environments, such as the fax room and the front seat of the Datsun). The last man I sexually harassed at work, I married so I could sexually harass him in the privacy of our own home.

In fact, seventy-five per cent of people meet their partners at work, or used to. If the next generation doesn't stop jumping on a chair and screaming 'Eek!' whenever a male colleague gets a whiff of their 'hook 'em and reel 'em in' perfume, they'll have no-one to consort with but their lawyers. Then we won't have famous workplace couplings such as Chairman and Madame Mao, Dawn French and Lenny Henry, Bill and Hilary Clint . . . Hmm, sometimes there *is* a case to answer.

Dear Doctor Jean,
I have anxious dreams about meeting Bill Clinton in the street and wondering whether to curtsy.
Francie, Fyshwick, ACT
Francie, never let your head get lower than his waist.

Crotch shots

You don't hear much about women's sport, apart from the shock discovery that Disprin won't shave precious seconds off your eight hundred metres.

Take two and you might be able to get out of bed after a tequila awareness party, but that's it.

Women's sport faces two problems: the media and the spectators. And I don't mean the tone of the media. Great strides, if you'll pardon the expression, have been made in newspaper reporting. Ten years ago if Melinda Gainsford and Kathy Freeman had been photographed sprinting to victory together, the headline would have read, 'What a Lovely Pair!' Not any more. Even sports editors have been retrained. One day even sports photographers won't always go for crotch shots in the jump events.

The real problem is getting coverage at all. But you only get coverage when you've got crowds of spectators. Most sports spectators are male. And there's a difference. Female spectators just like sport. Unlike men, they don't feel the need to see themselves out there, to believe that if they cut down on the smokes and ran around the block for a week, they too would force Carl Lewis to eat their shorts and dust. Men watch prime athletes twenty years younger in peak condition ripping ten seconds off a record or both ears off an opponent and think, 'That's me.' Put any six men together at a barbecue with a ball and you've got two scratch football teams, four beer bellies, two rooted knees and three coronaries.

Women's sport can't do this for men. So women's sport will have to appeal to other parts of their twelve-year-old imagination. What women's sport needs is more blood and more crime. When was the last time three players were carried off during a netball semi-final with their knee-caps in a lunchbox? Where's the women's hockey transfer scam? Where was the Super Netball legal triathlon?

Only when Australian women athletes make a commitment to damage people and property, and get suspended sentences, and be photographed coming out of courthouses in rented suits with dazed blonde fiancées, will Australian women's sport crash the front pages.

Only then will women's sport achieve equal opportunity, or as I like to put it, positive domination. Only then will women athletes be able to say, 'Stuff your breakfast cereals. I'm advertising big fat shoes. I'm the face of Gatorade.' Or knee wrinkle cream, anyway.

Dear Doctor Jean,

What gives women laugh lines around the eyes?

Carla, Elsternwick, Vic

Carla, the only time women on TV burst into face-creasing smiles of joy and wonder is when they think about washing powders or chat about Spamburgers, so I think the answer is either imbecility or drugs.

Ring of confidence

I have no objection to those women in advertisements who reach a state of ecstasy when their hair acquires bounce, or who smile radiantly while doing the shopping as if their neck tucks have seized. But there are some typecastings of women in commercials which really bring out the snarl in me.

The first is Executive Woman. In particular the woman who pretends to run the Panadol Empire. She wanders in, the guards salute, the scientists genuflect, and all the time you know, 'There is nothing in that briefcase, lady!' That is because women who run large enterprises do not wander around the shop like someone on Lithium who can't find the door. They take the lift to the boardroom, they kick off their shoes and they shout at the nearest flunkey, 'If I've got a headache, everyone has a headache. Sack the third floor.'

And if I'm going to buy their damn aspirin I want to see someone with a headache, I don't care how she got it. Whether she's got two children fighting over the remote control or whether she's spent all day trying to convince Panadol security she's not just another mad woman released into the community with a briefcase full of whoopee pills.

Then there's Soap Powder Woman. This evolving female seems to confuse the agencies mightily. They don't know whether to kit her out in a peg bag and trackies or a Brand Name suit and a digital phone. Who cares? I preferred the direct approach of the old days when women compared whiteness and one of them won. Get out your sheets and compete. Bring back Anne Deveson: teeth that had the ring of confidence and sheets from which the ring of husband had been erased. Today's soap powder ads ignore the one thing that all women know about washing: if it's annoying stains you're worried about they come from other people's annoying behaviour and the best answer is, 'That's a hand-washing job, you grub, do it yourself.' Let him bleach the wet spot.

But my principal beef, if you'll excuse the expression, is Worry Wart Women: the women-as-victims in the red meat cures iron deficiency commercials. This bunch of whingers wouldn't have iron deficiency if they hadn't fallen for the latest food scares perpetrated by female nutritionists in women's magazines. Food scares which are invariably contradicted in the next issue but one.

Twenty years ago the joke was that you could frighten a woman into squeals by shouting, 'Mice!' Now you can do it by shouting, 'Cholesterol!'

Remember when women weren't supposed to eat steak or drink red wine because we were too delicate? Then nutritionists said we shouldn't do it because it was bad for us? Then they discovered that red wine tidies up the cholesterol from a Scotch fillet and we had a balanced diet all along. But by then they had the problem of how to woo these female food neurotics back. So they came up with commercials which were also full of female food neurotics. Hah!

Whether women are seen having a coronary over a T-bone or falling unconscious over an iron deficient Salada they're victims. Nearly half the commercials shown on television are for food and if we want to restore female dignity we should stop grizzling about lingerie ads and put out a fatwah on Rosemary Stanton.

Innocent feminists argue that this problem can be fixed by smashing the glass ceiling, or having a little man come around and smash the glass ceiling. But can this problem really be fixed by more women making TV commercials? Or is this another argument like, 'Let's have more women in politics.' Because let's face it, when more women get into politics we fan out. We develop into more Margaret Thatchers and more Joan Kirners, more Benizir Bhuttos and Pauline Hansons and Bronwyn Bishops. Nothing in common but chromosomes. This is just as it should be.

And more women in advertising is just going to give us more Joan Singletons and more Greta Saatchis. They are still going to assure us that their products will cost less, taste better and remove stains. That their brand will fit more snugly, brake more comfortably in the wet, and absorb more blue liquid – for those women who have a biological urge to spill Windex once a month.

That will be their job. Meanwhile if they want to respond to the real lives of women, they might remember that women have husbands and fathers and sons, some of whom we chose. Ads do not enhance women by portraying these husbands as idiots who put OMO in the fridge or sons who have to be conned into eating breakfast cereal or fathers who have to be patronised into trying Tandoori lamb. Women are not empowered by people who dump on the men in our lives. We can dump on the men in our own lives without any help.

My daughter, Victoria, and her friends have work-shopped a new song which, I'm delighted to say, deals with gender-based interpersonal relationships and women's intuitive concern with diet.

> Boys go to Jupiter
> To make them more stupider
> Girls go to Mars
> To get more Mars bars.

I think they should apply for a grant.

Her women's song-cycle workshop has also come up with new songs to raise the consciousness of five-year-old women everywhere. My favourite recognises that women never have to explain themselves.

> Boys out, girls in,
> Not because they're dirty
> Not because they're clean
> Not because they kissed the girls behind the magazine.
> Just because.